S0-AGP-517

Cults

Other Books in the Social Issues Firsthand Series:

AIDS

Body Piercing and Tattoos

Child Abuse and Neglect

Date and Acquaintance Rape

Drunk Driving

Eating Disorders

Gangs

Prostitution

Sexual Predators

Teenage Pregnancy

Welfare

Cults

Doreen Piano, Book Editor

GREENHAVEN PRESS
A part of Gale, Cengage Learning

Detroit • New York • San Francisco • New Haven, Conn • Waterville, Maine • London

Christine Nasso, *Publisher*
Elizabeth Des Chenes, *Managing Editor*

For more information, contact:
Greenhaven Press
27500 Drake Rd.
Farmington Hills, MI 48331-3535
Or you can visit our Internet site at gale.cengage.com

Articles in Greenhaven Press anthologies are often edited for length to meet page requirements. In addition, original titles of these works are changed to clearly present the main thesis and to explicitly indicate the author's opinion. Every effort is made to ensure that Greenhaven Press accurately reflects the original intent of the authors. Every effort has been made to trace the owners of copyrighted material.

Cover photograph reproduced by permission of © Brooks Kraft/Sygma/Corbis.

LIBRARY OF CONGRESS CATALOGING-IN-PUBLICATION DATA

Cults / Doreen Piano, book editor.
p. cm. -- (Social issues firsthand)
Includes bibliographical references and index.
ISBN-13: 978-0-7377-4030-1 (hardcover)
ISBN-10: 0-7377-4030-2 (hardcover)
1. Cults. I. Piano, Doreen.
BP603.C845 2008
209--dc22

2008001707

Printed in the United States of America
2 3 4 5 6 7 12 11 10 09 08

Contents

Foreword

Social issues are often viewed in abstract terms. Pressing challenges such as poverty, homelessness, and addiction are viewed as problems to be defined and solved. Politicians, social scientists, and other experts engage in debates about the extent of the problems, their causes, and how best to remedy them. Often overlooked in these discussions is the human dimension of the issue. Behind every policy debate over poverty, homelessness, and substance abuse, for example, are real people struggling to make ends meet, to survive life on the streets, and to overcome addiction to drugs and alcohol. Their stories are ubiquitous and compelling. They are the stories of everyday people—perhaps your own family members or friends—and yet they rarely influence the debates taking place in state capitols, the national Congress, or the courts.

The disparity between the public debate and private experience of social issues is well illustrated by looking at the topic of poverty. Each year the U.S. Census Bureau establishes a poverty threshold. A household with an income below the threshold is defined as poor, while a household with an income above the threshold is considered able to live on a basic subsistence level. For example, in 2003 a family of two was considered poor if its income was less than $12,015; a family of four was defined as poor if its income was less than $18,810. Based on this system, the bureau estimates that 35.9 million Americans (12.5 percent of the population) lived below the poverty line in 2003, including 12.9 million children below the age of eighteen.

Commentators disagree about what these statistics mean. Social activists insist that the huge number of officially poor Americans translates into human suffering. Even many families that have incomes above the threshold, they maintain, are likely to be struggling to get by. Other commentators insist that the statistics exaggerate the problem of poverty in the United States. Compared to people in developing countries, they point out, most so-called poor families have a high quality of life. As stated by journalist Fidelis Iyebote, "Cars are owned by 70 percent of 'poor' households. . . . Color televisions belong to 97 percent of the 'poor' [and] videocassette recorders belong to nearly 75 percent. . . . Sixty-four percent have microwave ovens, half own a stereo system, and over a quarter possess an automatic dishwasher."

However, this debate over the poverty threshold and what it means is likely irrelevant to a person living in poverty. Simply put, poor people do not need the government to tell them whether they are poor. They can see it in the stack of bills they cannot pay. They are aware of it when they are forced to choose between paying rent or buying food for their children. They become painfully conscious of it when they lose their homes and are forced to live in their cars or on the streets. Indeed, the written stories of poor people define the meaning of poverty more vividly than a government bureaucracy could ever hope to. Narratives composed by the poor describe losing jobs due to injury or mental illness, depict horrific tales of childhood abuse and spousal violence, recount the loss of friends and family members. They evoke the slipping away of social supports and government assistance, the descent into substance abuse and addiction, the harsh realities of life on the streets. These are the perspectives on poverty that are too often omitted from discussions over the extent of the problem and how to solve it.

Greenhaven Press's Social Issues Firsthand series provides a forum for the often-overlooked human perspectives on society's most divisive topics of debate. Each volume focuses on one social issue and presents a collection of ten to sixteen narratives by those who have had personal involvement with the topic. Extra care has been taken to include a diverse range of perspectives. For example, in the volume on adoption, readers will find the stories of birth parents who have made an adoption plan, adoptive parents, and adoptees themselves. After exposure to these varied points of view, the reader will have a clearer understanding that adoption is an intense, emotional experience full of joyous highs and painful lows for all concerned.

The debate surrounding embryonic stem cell research illustrates the moral and ethical pressure that the public brings to bear on the scientific community. However, while nonexperts often criticize scientists for not considering the potential negative impact of their work, ironically the public's reaction against such discoveries can produce harmful results as well. For example, although the outcry against embryonic stem cell research in the United States has resulted in fewer embryos being destroyed, those with Parkinson's, such as actor Michael J. Fox, have argued that prohibiting the development of new stem cell lines ultimately will prevent a timely cure for the disease that is killing Fox and thousands of others.

Each book in the series contains several features that enhance its usefulness, including an in-depth introduction, an annotated table of contents, bibliographies for further research, a list of organizations to contact, and a thorough index. These elements—combined with the poignant voices of people touched by tragedy and triumph—make the Social Issues Firsthand series a valuable resource for research on today's topics of political discussion.

Introduction

The mass suicide of 914 members of the Peoples Temple in Jonestown, Guyana, in 1978 signaled a dangerous moment for many people who had been attracted to cults as an alternative to mainstream religions and lifestyles during the 1960s and 1970s. Despite the often liberating rhetoric offered by charismatic cult leaders like Jim Jones, many "doomsday" cults have a hidden apocalyptic aspect to them that emerges when a group perceives that it is being persecuted by outside forces. Since Jonestown, other cults have participated in group suicides, such as members of Heaven's Gate in 1997 and the Solar Temple in 1994, while some have directed violence toward their own societies. For example, in Japan, members of the cult known as Aum Shinrikyo deposited sarin gas at Tokyo subway stations, killing twelve and injuring thousands in 1995. Yet while doomsday cults often garner the most media attention due to their spectacular acts of violence, there are hundreds more worldwide that are barely noticed, functioning as microsocieties with their own internal organization, sets of rules, and beliefs and values that are often in opposition to the mainstream's. Because many cults incorporate aspects of established religions and can embody conventional religious beliefs, it can be difficult to differentiate a cult from a religion, and even more importantly to perceive when a cult is dangerous and whether or not its members are willingly adhering to what many view as an extreme lifestyle choice.

The Origin of the Term "Cult"

The term "cult" has been used since this "social problem" first manifested itself in the 1960s and 1970s and is still used by anticult and countercult organizations and activists such as the American Family Foundation and the Cult Awareness Network. Since the late 1990s, the term "new religious movements" (NRMs) has become more common among law enforcement, religious scholars, and sociologists to assign a less pejorative term to what is described as "young religious movements still in their first generation" that can encompass "New Age associations to Buddhist meditation groups to Christian premillennial movements."[1] To distinguish NRMs from more conventional religions, sociologists describe cults as "a movement that is foreign to the culture in which it lives."[2] Especially since the 1960s, the influence of non-Western religious movements such as The International Society for Krishna Consciousness (popularly known as Hare Krishnas), the Divine Light Mission, and the Unification Church became a source of anxiety and fear for many communities in the United States where these cults established themselves, attracting many white, middle-class youth to their alternative belief systems.

Many parents and former members define cults based on their techniques of brainwashing members, described by anticult organizations as "the belief that members of suspect groups ('cults') somehow had their cognitive capacities impaired through 'unethically manipulative methods' of persuasion."[3] Especially notable is the extreme measure of separating cult members from their families for lengthy periods of time, in addition to depriving members of food and/or sex, or from leaving freely. Besides forms of manipulation and persuasion, according to Margaret Thaler Singer, a leading anticult theorist, groups known as cults always have a charismatic leader and a hierarchical power structure that is often authoritarian. In fact, it is their strong sense of structure and devotion to utopian ideals that attract many young people to them.

The Allure and Danger of Cults

The centralized forms of power and psychological manipulation that cult leaders enforce lead many people to believe that those who join cults are easily duped or cannot be very intelligent. Interestingly enough, while it is true that cults tend to proselytize young people who are often looking for meaning in their lives or a need to separate from their families, many who join cults have a high IQ and are unusually creative and gifted. For many people, especially youth, cults offer an attractive outlet at a time in their lives when they may be questioning their own belief systems, looking for structure in their daily lives, or a sense of belonging separate from their families. The predominant view, however, is that cult members are brainwashed to remain in the organization through tactics that may involve physical deprivation, psychological manipulation, and sexual coercion. While manipulation appears to be a commonly used method, the strong structure that cults provide and their outsider ideology appeals to many young people who find mainstream society too confining or conventional religions lacking in zeal or relevance. However, even though "a cult's rules often are better defined than those of the family" which may provide a certain allure, joining a cult can lead to damaging effects such as identity loss and an obsessive devotion to a leader.[4]

When a cult actually becomes dangerous to society and/or its members is difficult to discern because many cults function on the periphery as a way of not calling attention to themselves. In the case of the Peoples Temple, the media and FBI's intense scrutiny of Jim Jones and his followers became an increasing source of disaffection and anger, which led Jones to move the Temple to the isolated jungles of Guyana in South America. For "catastrophic millennial groups" such as the Peoples Temple, a growing awareness of being persecuted by external forces reinforces the dualistic thinking that these cults foster among members, and can lead to violent encounters with authorities and/or mass suicide.[5]

Despite high-profile mass suicides and/or showdowns between cults and law enforcement, new cults continue to form globally, using new methods of recruitment such as the Internet. As Richard Lacayo writes, "It's persuasive, far reaching and clandestine. And for better and worse, it frees the imagination from the everyday world."[6] As cults continue to attract new members through their distinctive ideologies and dynamic leaders, more creative solutions need to be developed to educate those most vulnerable to cults' messages and to prevent cults from becoming violent. Additionally, many sociologists and law enforcement officials agree that regardless of the alienating features of cults that incite fear and anxiety, cult members should be treated as humanely as possible by creating a dialogue between cults and local officials and by monitoring their activities to safeguard both its members and the communities in which cults reside. Although some cults can be accused of horrible actions and tactics to maintain their membership, cult members will most likely eventually leave and assimilate into mainstream society. For most cult members, devoting their time to a particular cult is limited. In *Social Issues Firsthand: Cults* the authors provide a variety of personal accounts of their experiences with cults.

Notes

1. Adam Szubin, Carl Jensen, and Rod Gregg, "Interacting with 'Cults': A Policing Model," *FBI Law Enforcement Bulletin*. September 2000, p.17.
2. Ibid. p. 16.
3. Dereck Daschke and W. Michael Ashcraft, eds., *New Religious Movements: A Documentary Reader*. New York: New York University Press, 2005, p. 332.
4. Eagan Hunter, "Adolescent Attraction to Cults." *Adolescence*, Fall 1998.
5. Catherine Wessinger, *How the Millennium Comes Violently: From Jonestown to Heaven's Gate*. New York: Seven Bridges, 2000, p. 25.
6. Richard Lacayo, "The Lure of the Cult: Out Where Religion and Junk Culture Meet, Some New Offspring Are Rising," *Time*, April 7, 1997.

CHAPTER 1

Exploring Cults

What Kind of Person Joins a Cult?

Maureen Griffo

As an ex-member of The Church of Bible Understanding, Maureen Griffo understands what it is like to be in a cult and why someone would want to join. As she claims, anyone is vulnerable, including those who are highly intelligent and young. Writing this after the Heaven's Gate mass suicide in which all thirty-nine members died, Griffo discusses her own psychological experiences of being in a cult that included being financially bound to the group by signing over her paycheck. In addition, she shows the kinds of techniques that are used to keep members from rationally understanding how they are being manipulated. She adds, however, that reaching out to people who are in cults by being sympathetic rather than judgmental can make them see that people on the outside are friendly and willing to help, oftentimes more than their fellow cult members.

With the Heaven's Gate tragedy . . . certain questions seem to come up: What kind of person joins a cult? Why do they stay and put up with the abuse? How could anyone be *so* devoted that they would kill themselves? Can't they see that what they are doing is crazy? Are *they* crazy?

I feel that I am in a unique position to address these questions as I spent 10 years with a communal cult. Yet, now being out for 11 years, I also can look at the horrors that happened at Rancho Santa Fe [California] and ask, along with the rest of a stunned nation, "Why did they die like this?"

For eight and a half of the ten years I was with my former group, each payday I would sign my check over to the group. I would receive a meager allowance in return and would have to beg for the basics of life such as clothing and medical care.

Often I lived in substandard housing with rats, filth, and overcrowded conditions in neighborhoods with extremely high crime rates. After working a full day at work, I often would have to spend several hours on the street proselytizing. After returning, I would have to sit in meetings that lasted to the wee hours of the morning. These meetings were intense. Public humiliation was commonplace, and sometimes we would sit in silence for hours on end believing ourselves to be too reprobate even to speak. After getting an insufficient night's sleep, I would be expected to repeat the same routine of work and group activities all over again. In other words, there was no doubt that I was in a cult. Yet, if you had passed me in the street during the 10 years that I spent in the group, I can tell you that I wouldn't have been all that different from others in the crowd. My skin had not turned green, and I did not grow antennas. I had eyes, ears and a nose just like anyone else. I looked both ways before crossing a street. If somehow we got in an idle conversation that didn't involve my trying to recruit you, you may have been shocked to know that I had likes and dislikes just like any other person. I still liked pizza (even if I didn't have much access to it) and still hated pork sausage. Blue was still my favorite color, and I still loved sunsets. People who are in cults are just that—*people*—although sadly cults suppress much of what makes an individual unique. Heaven's Gate . . . forced all of us to come to grips with the realization that they were people not too unlike us, and that is indeed something tough to face. Whether one has been in a cult or not, the realization deep in our hearts that perhaps we could have shared a similar fate makes us want to turn away and believe that they had to be made of different stuff than we are. I am here to tell you that they are not.

Many Forms of Abuse

Why did the people in Heaven's Gate seem to go willingly to their deaths? Why did I stay in a clearly abusive situation for 10 years? The activities I felt trapped to do while within the group give some generous clues to how this can happen. And, when we can come to understand how one person can gain control over another, we can peer into the world of an average cult member. Indeed, one human being controlling another is nothing new to civilization. We need only look at the Biblical story of Cain and Abel to see the lengths that a person will go to in order to be "on top"—even if that means murder. It is no secret that sleep deprivation hinders clear thinking and decision making abilities. Through instituting a poor diet and strenuous routines, a group can break persons down further, making them even more vulnerable to the group's ideologies.

While the specific techniques may differ, almost every group has a way of inducing hypnosis. In my former group this was accomplished through the format of our meetings, which in reality were the focal point of what had become an intense system of peer scrutiny. Sitting in silence for hours affected me. I remember leaving many a meeting in which we had not spoken for hours with heaviness in my heart and feeling like my head had been put between two cymbals. Having to stand in front of my peers to be critiqued by them would seize me with panic. We would have to present ourselves one by one in front of a group of several hundred of our peers, stating what we did and where we were at in our hearts. The group would vote on us and the final vote became our guideline . . . it did not matter how we felt about things in our hearts. Often I was found to be deficient and would have to endure taunts by my peers between meetings. All of that was very intentional, coming from the leader himself and carried out through the ranks. There was no going home to escape all of this. I was home, and there was not a minute of privacy. I often could not think clearly and if I could get through a day feeling I held onto my sanity that was a major accomplishment.

Unable to Gain Any Critical Distance

My mind was too under siege to even think of packing my bags and leaving. This was purposeful as cults know that no one would make a rational decision to live like this and thus create an environment in which a person has no time or freedom to think. I have heard life in a cult compared to living in a fire constantly. Most of us can invoke images of people we've seen on the news who have lived through a fire. When persons are in the middle of a fire, they simply do not have access to certain parts of their thinking that they normally would have. However, when the fire is over, we see them collapse and say things like "Oh my God, I can't believe what happened. It was so terrifying." They are able to reconnect emotionally to their experiences and likely will be able to integrate what happened to them, thereby dealing with the trauma. Cults do not allow you to reconnect. I was kept so busy and off balance that the fire was never allowed to be over. Thus, outsiders could look at the way my fellow members and I lived in sheer horror; yet, while living in the midst of it, I simply could not get it. I get it now because I have been out, and as a person after a fire begins thinking again, I now have my critical thinking abilities back. Along with everyone else who hears about what happened to me, I am horrified to have spent 10 years of my life like that.

What could have been done to "reach" me during the 10 years I was in the communal group? What can we do to reach others who are in groups who may be heading down paths similar to that of Heaven's Gate or the other groups in recent times who have committed mass suicide? The biggest mistake people can make in reaching out to persons in a cult is forgetting that they are people too and that there are some logical reasons behind what on the surface appears to be bizarre behavior. If we remember that outside of the group's influences we would likely be dealing with a totally different person, he or she becomes less scary and more reachable to us. The dynamics of a cult are not too different from that of a battered wife staying with an abusive husband, or what happened in Nazi Germany or the Cultural Revolution in China. On the outside, they all seem to be beyond comprehension, but as we look at the underlying dynamics, their tactics are not that hard to understand. In our society today, all of us are being bombarded with huge amounts of information and people vying for our every dollar. Learning about techniques of influence and control can only benefit all of us as we are trying to navigate our way through an increasingly complex world. When it comes to understanding someone in a cult or other controlling situation, it can literally be life saving.

The people who had the biggest impact on me were not the ones who screamed at me "You're in a cult!" (Believe me, I had plenty of those.) Rather the ones who made me think were those willing to care about me as a person, whether I stayed or left. Despite their initial allure, cults do not offer unconditional love. When I saw people on the outside acting differently toward me than my own supposed all-loving peers, it affected me. I may not have left right away, but I could not shake that there was someone who would be willing to be my friend and care about me with no strings attached. Like anyone else faced with a decision, someone "decides" to join a cult based on the information available to him or her. Unfortunately, cults are notorious for not letting a potential recruit know about the full package. What I thought I was joining and what I actually joined were vastly different from each other. In other words, if the group had been up front about the kind of life I was going to have to live and what was going to happen to me, I would have never joined. . . .

Cults Go After the Best and Brightest

People in cults are not stupid. After leaving my former group, I was so convinced that I had to be intellectually deficient that I actually took an I.Q. test. Much to my surprise, instead of scoring way below average, I scored in the 97th percentile. As I have learned more about the kinds of people cults recruit, I have found that I am the rule and not the exception. Because the rigors of cult life are arduous, these groups do not want someone who will break down easily. Cults go after the best and the brightest—robbing all of us of people who could be making a huge difference in this world.

Who joins cults? They are anyone you could meet anywhere. I was a teen living in a small town when I had been recruited. I may have been naive and not able to see through the deception as someone older may have been, but most teens are naive and easily impressed by those who are slicker than themselves. I was not a drug addict or a prostitute, but rather I had been a good student in school who worked two jobs.

So, the next time you are approached by someone whom you strongly suspect may be living in a far out commune somewhere, remember you are likely to be dealing with a highly intelligent person who was deceived into joining what may appear to us as a bizarre cult. Instead of looking at such people as freaks or crazies, keep in mind that if they had access to more information and saw that there was a life outside for them, they probably would leave.

You Better Get Right with the Lord

Scott Schwartz

For several years, photographer and writer Scott Schwartz studied the religious ceremonies of an evangelical Christian church in eastern Kentucky. More commonly known as serpent-handlers, those involved in this church interpret the Bible literally, and their ceremonies include unorthodox rituals such as the handling of deadly snakes, rhythmic chanting and music, speaking in tongues, and exposing themselves to fire. While to many people these rituals may appear bizarre and dangerous, as Schwartz's reporting reveals, they are also compelling enough for nonbelievers to be persuaded by the intensity of the experience. In this excerpt, Schwartz writes about witnessing the ceremonies surrounding this eclectic religious community with compassion. He takes the reader through the details of the ceremony step by step, showing the powerful trancelike state that the participants fall into as part of their religious beliefs.

The trip is familiar—left at Duffield, right to Pennington Gap, and right again to Harlan, Kentucky. Route 421 is the worst part of the drive. It snakes through Virginia's and Kentucky's mountains past one-stop gas marts, red brick houses, abandoned coal tipples, and three small faded crosses nailed to a tree. The sun is sliding behind the mountains. Approaching the final hairpin curve into Crummies, Kentucky, I switch on the headlights and look up from the dashboard just in time to avoid hitting a coal truck doing some overtime.

I pull into the church's small parking lot, and the preacher's wife, Valerie, waves to me as she walks into the

Scott Schwartz, *Faith, Serpents, and Fire: Images of Kentucky Holiness Believers*, Jackson, MS: University Press of Mississippi, 1999, pp. 5–25.

church. The white cinder-block-and-wood building stands next to a row of redbud trees that have been stripped of their weathered leaves by January's unrelenting winds. I take in a deep breath and think to myself, "Kentucky is a much prettier place in the spring."

I'm greeted by the familiar odor of blazing kerosene heaters as I walk through the front door. Bags of recording and photographic equipment hang from my shoulders like giant supply sacks and make me look like a yuppie peddler. I shake hands with several of my new friends and sit down in a worn wooden pew. Biblical quotations, a wooden cross, and images of Christ are carefully displayed on each wall. Only a phosphorus-colored clock with the word "Squirt" stenciled across its face seems out of place. Kerosene-filled Coke bottles, a propane torch, and a bottle of olive oil have been set on the pulpit. A worn Bible is opened to Mark 16, verses 17–18, in preparation for the night's salvation. Handcrafted boxes lie beneath the front pew, and a sporadic buzzing is the only hint of the serpents inside. Nothing has changed since last month's visit.

As I begin setting up equipment, my mind drifts for a moment. Why am I doing this? The answer comes to me in a flash of images as I open up my tripod. Men and women greeting each other as brother and sister in the church's dusty parking lot, the men exchanging handshakes, the women herding the children into the meeting house, sitting down next to the serpent boxes, and showing one another the latest photographs of their children and grandchildren. Sherman standing outside the church talking with Gary and Wayne about hunting deer with his son in Boone County on a sunny afternoon. Kimberly taking a well-practiced snap of a hickory switch to her son's backside to stop him from running inside the church. A young girl sitting next to her sister and flirting with some pubescent boys. Everything seems so natural; yet the media's blitz about a recent serpent-handling fatality paints a much darker and more sinister picture of these people. However, I am drawn by a brighter image.

The Service Begins

No one seems to notice that I'm back for the Saturday service. Reaching for my video camera, I notice a tired-looking man sitting with his two daughters, one sleeping next to him and the other merrily chattering to her grandmother. Jesus's name is tattooed across the knuckles of his left hand, the tattoo having been created with blue ink and a nail.

I look at my watch and notice that it is 7:06 p.m. Gary and Wayne have settled down behind the pulpit, tuning their guitars. Matt picks a finger-blazing "rift" aimed at no one in particular; it screams through the speakers, "I've got a new gospel song to play tonight when the spirit moves on me." The electric bass player is unmoved by Matt's gymnastic display and sits quietly replacing a broken string.

At 7:10 there is still no visible sign that anyone has come to church tonight for a serpent- and fire-handling service. Sherman plays half a verse of "Amazing Grace" and, stopping abruptly, asks for the remaining changes. I reach for my note log and start counting—five men, eight women, and eleven children. Sherman walks up to the microphone, casually telling everyone that "it's time to begin—it's time to get your minds on the Lord." Without a further word, the men and women kneel next to their seats. The children briefly stop their playful antics and watch the familiar scene unfold once again.

People begin praying with their faces buried in their hands, the voices resonating throughout the room. I wonder why they do this, and make a note to ask Bruce after the service. It's a wonderful chorus of *sprechstimmen* [spoken singing] that rises from the pews and fills the room with an otherworldly sound, at once melodic and staccato, and I find myself drawn to it. "Hallelujah—THANK YOU, JESUS!" comes from somewhere. Was that me or Sherman who just shouted? The service has begun, and I note the time.

The Room Feels Electrified

Sherman slowly stands up from his kneeling position and walks again to the microphone. A six-string guitar now hangs from his shoulder as he silently watches the last of the praying. A hush falls over the meeting as all return to their seats. Sherman sings, "Amaaaaaazzzzing Gracccccce, how SWEEEEEEET the SOOOOOOOOUUUUND," and the rest of the members begin to join in. His tempo is slow and self-assured, as if the gospel song were a majestic march promising to lead its followers to Heaven's gateway. Everyone's attention is drawn to the preacher, and the anticipation of something spiritual brings an almost electric feeling to the room. Without warning, the pent-up energy of the entire congregation explodes in a frenzy of dancing, rattling tambourines, and clanging cymbals as Sherman speeds through the remaining verses in double time. "Amazing Grace, how sweet the sound to save a wretch like me."

The rhythmic pulse of the overly amplified electric bass pounds my chest; the music's volume is deafening. The music is a rousing mixture of gospel, blues, country, and rock and roll. Its spell pulls me toward the light of the service. I'm clapping and singing along with the others. I stop, hurriedly grab my notepad, and scribble down some inconsequential observations in a futile effort to retain some scholarly composure. The Holy Spirit is infectious; I feel its presence throughout the room.

Sherman's son, Matt, walks up to the microphone just as his father finishes the song. He spiritedly sings, "I ain't got no time for you, Devil." My attention is immediately yanked away from the notepad as his mother shouts, "THANK YOU, JESUS—HELP HIM, LORD!" Brenda relinquishes her tambourine to Valerie and begins convulsing around the room like a rag doll puppet, wildly pulled this way and that by the Holy Spirit's strings. She suddenly stops and places her hands on Melissa's forehead, speaking in "unknown tongues." I note the time of the service's first spiritual anointing. Gary and Sherman start jumping up and down, and the room's activities are now chaotic. I can barely keep up with the frenzied activities as I take photographs. I wonder, is the music driving the service or is the Holy Spirit propelling the music?

Snakes Appear

It seems like only a second has passed since I last looked up from my notepad, and now Wayne is carrying three big black serpents, each as thick as a man's forearm. Sherman reaches into a box behind the pulpit and pulls out a smaller one. He raises the serpent above his head and fearlessly stares straight into its coal-black eyes. Kimberly walks to the front of the church and gently handles a big reptile with her husband, Gary. Sherman ignites a kerosene-filled Coke bottle and continues to jump up and down. The floor shakes with each bounce, and the flames from the kerosene lamp lick his perspiration-soaked chin. He passes the serpent to Wayne. From the back of the church, Wayne's two daughters strain to get a better view of their father. Their mother, Sheila, restrains them for their own protection. Note taking is futile; I just sit and watch the activities, dumbfounded.

Contemplating the night's events, I notice a blond-headed boy, Paul, standing on the pew next to me. He's mesmerized just as I am. All of a sudden two young boys climb over the row of seats in front of us and wrestle Paul to the floor. A hickory switch blurs in front of me, and I'm abruptly brought back to reality. I pick up my camera again and snap a photograph of Cody standing by himself and playing with a toy rubber snake, imitating his father's serpent handling at the front of the church. Brook is holding Sherman's hand now and vigorously rattling her tambourine. Her blond pigtails bounce in time with the music.

I suddenly realize that Bruce has taken the microphone and is propelling the gathering with another song. The different elements of the service are beginning to blur together. Now Bruce is handling serpents, and Mark is quietly sitting on the sidelines running the flame from the kerosene-filled Coke bottle under his hand. His wife and daughter sit next to him and watch. A single sixty-watt light bulb eerily illuminates the room, bathing everyone in a purifying light. Buffy, Brenda, and Valerie are now singing Dorothy Eldridge's "He Is Jehovah." Buffy's lead is natural as she reaches into the depths of her inner spirit to bring a personal message to the service. Her voice is a gutsy mixture of Joshua Redman soul and Alison Krauss country. The sound is pure platinum.

Michelle is feeding Gerber's chicken noodle dinner to her son Nathan at the back of the church, as if they were on a spring picnic. Marshall is talking intimately with Brenda's daughter, their heads gently touching. Sherman's hands are engulfed in the flames of another kerosene-filled Coke bottle that is on the pulpit. Kimberly sits in quiet reflection. Sherman's mother, Bertha, standing next to the front door, is experiencing a gentler form of the Holy Spirit. Gail's anguished expression of the spiritual experience is oddly reflected in her tears of joy. The sweat pours from Sherman's forehead and Gary's once neatly pressed shirt is now soaked and untucked. The music continues to pound my chest, and goose bumps shoot up my spine.

Without warning, Valerie walks to the back of the church and climbs over several individuals in an effort to reach me. She's on a quest, and there is no turning back. She places her cold hand on my forehead and begins speaking: "Sha-la-la-la-la-na-na help him, Lord, to see the way, sha-la-la-la-la-la-na-na-na." The music suddenly stops and everyone's attention goes to the back of the church. Sitting perfectly still, my ears burning, I try to remember why I started this research, noting to myself that they hadn't mentioned anything like this to me when I was in graduate school. The room is deadly still as Valerie continues to speak in tongues. "HELP HER, SWEET JESUS" comes from the front of the church, but I don't look up, fearful of disturbing the moment. "Sha-la-lala-la-na-na help him, Lord, to see the way, help us teach him the way of the Lord."

As suddenly as the service began, it stops. It's the halftime break of a spiritual event in which the contestants are saints and sinners, and the prize is salvation. Sherman walks to the cooler to fill up his paper cup with water. Valerie pulls some Kleenex from a box on the pulpit and wipes her forehead. Wayne takes his daughter, Samantha, to the bathroom. Oddly, my heart is still pounding, and my ears continue to burn. Several of the women are sitting on the front pew combing their hair and drying their faces with a white towel. The mood is almost jovial. Gary crosses the room and slaps Sherman on the back, proudly stating, "The Spirit is really with us tonight." "Yes, the Spirit is with us tonight, Brother Gary," says Sherman. "Why don't you do the reading for us, Brother Gary?"

"You Better Get Right with the Lord."

Without further prompting, Gary walks to the pulpit and grabs both sides of it with his hands. He begins the sermon by reading Mark 16:17–18: "And these signs shall follow them that believe; In my name shall they cast out devils; they shall speak with new tongues; They shall take up serpents; and if they drink any deadly thing, it shall not hurt them; they shall lay hands on the sick, and they shall recover." Gary pauses briefly, takes in a deep breath, and then, looking up from the biblical scripture, points a finger directly at me and says, "You better get right with God, because the Day of Judgment is near." As I quietly stare back at Gary, I remind myself that there's no way of avoiding the direction of tonight's sermon. I'm going to be its focus. So much for playing the role of an unobtrusive observer.

Gary's sermon consists of short extemporaneous phrases, each punctuated with a violent exhalation, the combination of which creates a perpetual asymmetrical pattern of sounds. It was the same pattern that I had heard on many past visits. "You better get right with the Lord—ha!, because the Day of Judgment is near—ha!, if you don't see the light, Brother Sherman—ha!, you're never goin' receive the keys to the Almighty Kingdom—ha!, you better get right with the Lord—ha!, because if you don't you're goin' to burn in Hell's almighty fire—ha!, you never felt a fire like this, Brother Sherman—ha!, not everyone is goin' to Heaven, Brother Sherman—ha!, but I know I'm goin' to Heaven, because I'm right with the Lord—ha!, the Lord isn't goin' to let just anyone into Heaven, Brother Sherman—ha!, and you can bet that some of us here tonight aren't goin' to be standin' at the Pearly Gates when Judgment Day comes—ha!" "HELP HIM, SWEET JESUS" comes from somewhere at the front of the church, and Gary slaps his hand down on the Bible and continues his feverish pitch. "You better get right with God—ha!, because the JUDGMENT DAY IS NEAR—YES, IT IS!"

The sermon is mind numbing, so I reach for my log and start scribbling thoughts about the night's service. As I become engrossed in my note taking, Gary's sermon fades into a distant drone, and for a few minutes I find my thoughts drifting freely. As I look up from my notebook, I notice that Valerie is sitting at the front of the church fanning herself with a piece of paper. She also appears to be lost in some distant thought. Her daughter Melissa is sitting next to her, and is rocking her own daughter, Jessica, to sleep. Wayne walks back into the church with Samantha and takes a seat next to his wife, Sheila. Katrina watches her brother Cody play with the cymbals, giving him a look that any sister would give to a brother. When I turn my attention back to the pulpit, Sherman is giving the sermon, the subject of which is now serpent handling; I am no longer the focus. I whisper to myself, "Thank God for small miracles, Maybe the Spirit does work in mysterious ways."

Real Time and Spiritual Time Blurs

The clock reads 8:45, and there's no sign of an end to the sermon. The communion and foot washing are going to extend the service well beyond 9:00 this evening. I hope that I can stay awake for the long drive home tonight. No sooner do I note the time in my log than the sermon is finished. Gary and Sherman are carrying a small wooden table and two chairs to the center of the room, and everything seems improvisatory. I wonder whether this is the case with every communion and foot washing. I note the time as 8:57, but I'm no longer sure what is real time and what is spiritual time. Saltine crackers have been broken up and placed on a paper plate and a glass of blood-red wine has been poured from an unlabeled gallon jug.

Sherman and Gary lift up the goblet of wine and plate of crackers and pray, "Thank you, sweet Jesus, for the food that we're about to take." The mood again is jovial, with Valerie and Brenda sitting at the table as if it were a Sunday afternoon dinner. They gently retrieve a piece of cracker from the sacramental plate, then bow their heads as Sherman and Gary recite: "Take this bread, for it is the body of Christ, and drink this wine, for it is the blood of Christ." They quickly chew their saltine wafers and take a sip from the plastic chalice. Brenda looks up and smiles. Valerie wipes away tears of joy with the palms of her hands. The scene is repeated as first the women are served and then the men.

The children are last, and Gary's eight-year-old son, Adam, sits proudly in the place of honor. It's his first communion, and he clearly likes the attention. He mimics exactly what he saw his father and mother do a few minutes earlier. The cracker goes down with a smile, but the wine elicits a pained expression, and he sputters, "I thought this was going to taste like grape juice." Adam wipes his tongue with his shirt sleeve, and everyone starts laughing.

The Men Begin Washing Their Feet

Without a further word, Wayne begins hanging a cloth from a metal clothesline that has been stretched right down the middle of the church. As Sherman and Gary move the communion table and chairs behind the pulpit, Wayne carefully attaches wooden clothespins to the handmade blanket, and I ask Sherman why this is being done. He smiles and says, "Men and women are not permitted to wash each other's feet in public. The blanket separates us during the footwashing. You'll have to remain on this side of the blanket with the men." As I give Sherman an understanding nod, I notice Gary pulling some clear plastic gallon jugs filled with water from under the front pew. Wayne hands out a plastic wash basin and a couple of towels to the women on the other side of the blanket wall. Sherman sits down on one of the pews and begins taking off his shoes and socks. He looks up at me and says, "Foot washing teaches us humility. Would you like to join us?"

I politely excuse myself from the activity by suggesting that I need to stand on the back pew to get a better angle for my photographs. Everyone has bare feet, as if it were a sweltering August afternoon, even though the temperature outside is well below freezing. The heaters, however, keep us warm and comfortable.

Sherman places his feet in the basin of water. The rest of the men kneel around him and begin washing his feet. He leans his large frame back and reaches his arms skyward as if trying to touch the Holy Spirit. "THANK YOU, SWEET JESUS; ooooooh thank you, thank you, Jesus." His eyes are transfixed on something in the distance, and a tear begins a gentle descent down his fleshy cheek. Giggles come from the other side of the blanket, and suddenly someone shouts, "SHA-LA-LA-LA-NA-NA-NA," and then begins to cry. Brook peeks her head from behind the cloth wall and flashes her father a sheepish grin before disappearing behind the blanket again. I turn my attention back to Sherman, and, just as I take his photograph, I say to myself, "If I didn't know better I would think he has actually been touched by the Holy Spirit." There's a special glow surrounding his face as I snap his picture, and I turn the camera around to see if I've smudged the lens, but it's perfectly clean. I rub the exhaustion from my eyes. It's been a long night.

The foot washing ritual is repeated for each of the men, and I note that it has been nearly thirty minutes since the beginning of this final part of the service. As Gary and Sherman dry their feet, Adam runs from behind the blankets and takes a seat beside the basin. Without any coaching from his father, he places his feet into the basin and stands up. His hands are raised above his head as his father's had been a few moments before. The men kneel and start washing his feet, and a broad smile flashes across his face.

Satan Came Knocking

The men finish their foot washing several minutes before the women do and begin to put on their shoes. They laugh quietly in response to the women's continued wails and cries from the other side of the cloth wall. Adam is sitting proudly next to his father drying his feet. A toothy smile again beams from his devilish face, and I can't stop myself from taking another photograph. He's the center of attention and knows it. Sherman walks to the blanket and says, "Valerie, are you almost done?" In a hushed voiced she responds, "In a minute—okay?"

The service comes to a close as the blanket is taken down and everyone is refreshed. The talk is about Sunday's service at Jamie's church in Middlesboro and how well the spirit moved on the service tonight. Wayne stands next to the front door holding Jessica in his arms, and it's hard for me to recognize him as the same man who handled serpents during the service a couple of hours ago. Sherman smiles at me and says, "Yes, the Spirit really moved on us tonight—would you like to come to the house for some coffee before you head home?" Gary, who hands Wayne a box of serpents as he heads out the front door, says, "The Spirit really did move on us tonight. Satan came knocking on the church door and the Spirit just sent him packin'—won't you come on up to the house for a little while? We can talk." I am bone tired and say that I need to head home right away, since it's getting pretty late. I thank everyone for inviting me to the evening's service and tell them that I'm looking forward to returning next month. As I shake hands with Valerie, she says "You come back any time; you're just like one of the family."

Burning Man

Vendela Vida

Started in the 1980s by Larry Harvey, the Burning Man Festival, which began in San Francisco and subsequently moved to Black Rock Desert in Nevada, has become an annual event in which a towering effigy is constructed and then destroyed at the end of the festival. Each year thousands of people descend upon the fabricated city of Black Rock to honor the Man and to temporarily enjoy a total escape from the structure and obligations of everyday life. In this chapter from her book about young women's coming-of-age experiences, Vendela Vida traveled to the Nevada desert to participate in the Burning Man experience. Foremost in her mind is to find out what exactly draws people to go to Burning Man Festival and what happens. Additionally, she decides to join in as much as possible to gain a full understanding of this communal event.

I am standing in the middle of a Nevada desert on the Sunday of Labor Day weekend amid fifteen thousand people—many of them naked—who dance, drum, and cheer as a forty-foot neon-tube-outlined wooden effigy of a man is set on fire. Some people shake rubber chickens at the Man, others throw women's lace underwear in his direction, one guy places a pizza box at the Man's feet, or rather, where his feet would be if he had extremities, and almost everyone chants "Burn him!" The crowd's passion (what has this expressionless stick figure ever done to them?) and energy (this night is the culmination of what for some has been a four-day orgy of drinking, drugging, and dancing) is unlike anything I have ever witnessed (and during the past few days I've seen *plenty*). It was to understand what inspired this passion, energy, and growing de-

Vendela Vida, *Girls on the Verge: Debutante Dips, Drive-bys, and Other Initiations*, Basingstoke, Hampshire: St. Martin's Press, 1999, pp. 137–170.

votion to a ritual whose meaning is unstated and open to personal interpretation—a ritual with no determined significance?—that I ventured to the 1997 Burning Man festival.

Many things about the annual Burning Man have changed in the dozen years since its inception on a San Francisco beach—the time (originally it took place in June in honor of the summer solstice); the place (it's moved from the aforementioned beach to the Nevada desert); the size of the effigy (the Man has grown from eight feet to forty); the length of the event (instead of a one-night festivity, it now spans the course of an entire long weekend, plus); and the number of attendees (the count's gone from twenty to fifteen thousand). One thing that has not altered is that Burning Man-ners—devotees who make the trek from around the world every year to watch the Man burn—maintain that the ritual provides their lives with something missing from their everyday existence: community.

Having grown up in San Francisco, I'd been hearing about Burning Man for years. It always had an aura of the primitive. I was intrigued by the ritual of it, by the focus on fire, by the fact that no matter how many people I asked I could never get a very clear idea of what it was all about. I'd never seriously considered making the trek to the desert myself, but the summer of 1997 was different. My research for this book had led me to discussions with young women about their experiences belonging to a group and I had begun to get a sense of the needs which compel so many people to be a part of some community. As for myself, I was unaffiliated and increasingly disconnected, more so because of my discovery that everyone else seemed to be affiliated/connected/communitized. Even my friends. Unlike them, I didn't belong to a church/synagogue/mosque, a softball team, the Junior League, a yoga institute, a reading circle, a tennis ladder, a CD club, the Yeats society, or AA [Alcoholics Anonymous].

As I began to acknowledge my status as a non-community member, Burning Man took on a new appeal. I imagined that if the world was tilted on its axis, everyone who wasn't tied down to a community would slide into Black Rock City, as Burning Man-ners have christened their Arcadia. And so I went to Burning Man to investigate if, after all, there was a place for people like me; I went to Burning Man wondering if something totally transformative would occur and I would come away from it with a new Sense of Belonging.

Heading to Black Rock City

To get to Burning Man I flew from New York to San Francisco and met up with my younger sister, Vanessa. Vanessa is a psychology major at [the University of California at] Berkeley whose motivations for going to Burning Man were totally different from mine. Initially, I was surprised she wanted to accompany me on my trek. Her reasons? "I'm reading [Sigmund] Freud's *Civilization and Its Discontents* and I was thinking that, well, isn't Burning Man a civilization created by discontents?

"Plus," she continued, "these really cute guys who sit behind me in Developmental Psychopathology were talking about how they're going. I'm *there*."

So on the Thursday evening before Labor Day weekend, our trunk packed with camping equipment and our glove compartment stuffed with maps, directions, and various Burning Man "survival guide" tips we've been sent in the mail along with our tickets, we head off from San Francisco for Black Rock City. After driving East for four hours we stop at a Sak 'N Save on the outskirts of Reno.

We've just begun filling up our cart with the two gallons of water per person per day recommended in the Burning Man survival kit when some Teva-footed and Patagonia-clad people in Aisle 4 who are volleyballing a Sak 'N Save pink beach ball between them say, "Burning Man?"

"How'd you know?" I ask.

Green Patagonia spikes the ball and then nods at our water jug stacked shopping cart. Our cart is full, but when we join the checkout line it appears we're a bit understocked for Burning Man. Like Vanessa and me, the couple in front of us has a shopping cart with water bottles practically toppling out. Unlike us, they have another cart packed with Sam Adams's, Jack Daniels, Smirnoff, Marlboros, and Advil. The group of guys in back of us have two carts, both loaded with beer. On the bottom rack of one cart are several ice blocks the size of laundry bags. On the bottom rack of the other sit three inflated pink beach balls. I feel as though I've got a big sticker on my butt that says "Burning Man Virgin."

The checkout boy is pimply and nervous, Central Casting's night shift supermarket boy. He asks where we're heading and tells us that he only knows about Burning Man because one time he and his friends were driving through the desert and they came across a forty-foot man. "We didn't know what the heck was going on," he says. "It was really weird."

At the Epicenter of an All-Night Bacchanalia

It's well after midnight and we've been driving in the dark in what looks like post-apocalyptic terrain—it's just been us and the tumbleweed—when suddenly an illuminated metropolis rises up before us like the Emerald City in *The Wizard of Oz.* I had imagined Black Rock City would look like a very big campground—a bunch of tents, portable stoves, and flashlights—but instead trailers, RVs with satellite dishes, and rotating searchlights abound. And there, in the center of it all, stands a neon blue figure in the shape of a man. We've arrived.

Halfway down the road that leads to the start of the city, a harelipped woman with a coal miner's light on her head waves us down, takes our tickets, and hands us a map of Black Rock City. Like a real city, Black Rock has streets, a city center, and suburbs. A surveyor designs the city around the focal point so that the streets are essentially concentric circles around the Man—one circle outside another, like a dart board. Acting as though we are on a quest for the heart of darkness, we head straight downtown, toward the Man himself.

"To describe Burning Man, the great upwelling of creative energy that occurs in the Nevada desert every year preceding Labor Day, is like describing the abundance—the sheer, prodigal, and superfluous fertility—of Nature itself," reads the first paragraph of a pamphlet about Burning Man that I received in the mail with my tickets and survival guide. But when we arrive at an empty campsite in downtown Black Rock—we're directed there by a drunk guy on a bike with a painted-blue face—we step out of the car and into pounding techno music. This is a rather unusual Nature. The only sense in which I'm experiencing a return to primitive conditions is that I feel like I'm in the epicenter of a fifteen thousand-person all-night Bacchanalia.

Vanessa and I have traveled to villages without electricity in Third World countries, we've gone alone to places where guidebooks strongly advise against women traveling without male accompaniment, and yet upon our arrival at Burning Man, I feel as though we've just arrived in the center of [Dutch painter] Hieronymus Bosch's *Garden of Earthly Delights*. Various camps have improvised a battle of the bands (that is, a struggle to assert the superiority of their taste in music merely by playing it at the highest decibel), and the resulting cacophony makes the Tower of Babel seem positively peaceful. Everyone is in various states of both undress and advancement in their drug enhancement/impairment programs, and there appears to exist an inverse relationship between the former and the latter: The greater the drug intake, the scarcer the clothing. . . . Frankly, we're scared. It's one o'clock and we decide to wait until the sun's out to set up our tent; we lower the car seats, lock the car doors, and sleep.

The Barbie Camp

When I wake up in the car the next morning the first person I see through the window is a naked woman. What's more bizarre than waking up to nude strangers is how quickly one becomes accustomed to seeing nude strangers. After Vanessa and I set up the tent, we start walking around Black Rock City and it takes less than an hour for me to become fairly oblivious to who's naked and who's not. Sometimes I just notice people's body pierces (seeing naked people makes you realize how many places there are on your body for unusual pierces). Neither gender nor body type prevents people from showing all they've got, and I find it interesting to see how many places there are on a body for fat deposits—I even see a guy with a fat spine. From a distance, I often think people are clothed, only to discover as we approach that they've just painted clothes on—bikini tops, shorts, shirts, even G-string underwear.

The male/female ratio at Burning Man is roughly even, and the average age of the attendees is twenty-seven, with most being between eighteen and forty. There is, of course, the occasional couple in their sixties, and surprisingly, a lot of kids. The kids spend most of their time doing roughly what the adults are doing—riding around on their bikes, dancing, talking to people—but unlike in Society, it's the adults who are naked and the kids who are clothed. One eight-year-old girl we meet named Marjorie has a banana bike with her, but she tells us she's only allowed to ride it "around the block." "I keep an eye on my dad's Camp Barbie," she says. "You want to see?"

Like a carnival with lots of booths, Burning Man comprises camps, which many people have spent a lot of money and time preparing. We follow Marjorie to her father's camp, a display of about thirty Barbies, all of which are mutated in some way. "I helped him make that one," she says, and she points to a hirsute Barbie. "I glued the hair on its back." This,

I think, is what separates a Burning Man kid from a normal cute blond suburban girl on a banana bike: she derives great pleasure and a humongous missing-a-couple-of-teeth smile from deforming dolls, and she refers to Barbie as an "it."

Innuendo, Puns, and Weirdos

In some ways Burning Man is made for kids, what with the mud and the games and the bikes. But in other respects it seems entirely wrong because a large percentage of the camps have sex-based themes. There's a confession booth for telling stories about something that made you laugh in bed, and some women walk around on stilts wearing to-the-knee dildos and shouting "Show us your cocks" to all the men in the vicinity.

We pass a camp with a sign saying "Leave your shoes at the door and come in and wash your souls." Another camp features scantily clad women who ask if you want to get laid, and regardless of your response, bedeck you with plastic leis. "What's up with the puns?" Vanessa says, as a woman walks by us with a big plastic hammer and says "Get hammered" to everyone she encounters, before bopping them on the head.

Puns, in fact, abound at Burning Man—perhaps because they provide an easy entré into interaction; they make it seem as though everyone's privy to the same punchline of a joke. "This is so lame," Vanessa says. "Everything is not funny. Okay, maybe the first time, but after the hundredth time—no, scratch that—after the fifth time it's just pathetic. Who are these people?" She tells me she wants to go back to our camp and read; I agree to meet her there at three o'clock. I want to yell something protective after her like "Don't talk to any weirdos," but I refrain because at Burning Man this is essentially impossible.

Participants, Not Spectators, Welcome

Sisterless, I am left standing in front of Temps Perdu, the big cafe in the center of Black Rock City. The cafe has haystacks and tables and, improbably, an espresso machine. Stretched across the width of the cafe's partial roof is a banner that reads, "No Spectators."

The "no spectators" refrain is a popular one at Burning Man. According to Larry Harvey, one of the event's founding fathers, Burning Man is an alternative to the TV-watching culture of America. Therefore, everyone should be a participant. Participants are good, spectators bad, and the distinction between the two groups is not insubstantial. Spectators suffer a fate worse than that of high school outcasts: They're taunted, sneered at, and abused by the "in" crowd, i.e., the elite, the participants. The media are considered the biggest spectators around and it's par for the course that Burning Man participants clank bells into news reporters' microphones and/or squirt water directly at their video camera lenses while announcing, "This is Media Interference."

Some participants have spent a good part of the year conceiving an idea for a theme camp and saving up for U-Hauls and RVs to transport all the necessary theme-camp furnishings to Burning Man. This type of participant makes up about 50 percent of Burning Man's population; another 25 percent is made up of the sort of participants who run around on acid, Ecstasy, 'shrooms or pot, taking part in (those doing pot or Ecstasy) or freaking out about (those on acid and 'shrooms) the aforementioned participants' creations.

Despite all the professed animosity toward their kind, the remaining 25 percent of Black Rock City is made up of spectators. Even the people sitting on haystacks underneath the "No Spectators" banner are spectators. Sipping cappuccinos from the cafe, they read the Black Rock Gazette (Burning Man's daily newspaper) while listening to 99.5 (Burning Man's radio station). Their primary pastime, however, seems to be sitting and watching all the weird people who pass by. Some spectators even film the participants with video cameras so that they can watch them on TV when they get home.

Attending the Sunscreen Camp

The general consensus is that being a participant is the only way to fully experience Burning Man. Although I haven't brought anything to share with anyone else, my desire to be initiated into the world of participants—and thereby discover a Sense of Belonging—leads me to the Sunscreen Camp. To keep the heat of the desert away from pale skin, some opt for parasols, others for strategically placed Band-Aids. Most go the sunscreen route, however, and this is one of the reasons the Sunscreen Camp is so popular. The Sunscreen Camp is shaded by a large canopy, and beneath it are two massage tables, a tub of sunscreen, and ten volunteer sunscreeners. The camp's motto, as stated on a large banner, is "Burn the Man, Not Your Body."

Wendy, a storklike woman with bright eyes and prominent ribs who's (only) wearing men's BVDs tells me she started the camp after coming to Burning Man last year and seeing all the burned bodies by the end of the event. "The camp's turning out to be quite popular," Wendy says with pride, as though she's an entrepreneur whose company has just gone public. "We've had constant lines and more than enough volunteers."

A line of eight people are waiting for a massage—among them, a naked man, the naked man's clothed five-year-old son, three naked women, and a couple who just got married the night before beneath the Man. When it's my turn to get sunscreened I lay on my stomach on a table and think, This is all for free! Never would this happen in Society, never would this happen to my friends who frequent spas. Three (three!) volunteer masseuses/sunscreeners get to work on me—one on my right foot, one on my back, and one on my arms.

The guy who's massaging my foot twists it slowly in all sorts of strange directions. I've never really believed foot fetishists existed beyond the personal ads in the *Village Voice*, but this guy makes me wonder. A theatrical set designer from Houston, he tells me that his dream is to one day do the design for the set of *Alice in Wonderland.* "I want to do everything—the set, the mushroom, the costumes," he says as he enthusiastically rubs lotion between my second and third toes. "I saw a production of it last year and the whole thing was wrong. I mean, the guy's vision was so far off it was unbelievable. I've never seen anyone do a good *Alice.* With my vision, I have to do it. No one even pictures Alice the way I do."

"How do you picture her?" I ask.

"In high stiletto heels," he says.

The guy who's doing my back rubs lotion in with one hand and uses the other to draw shapes. For a few minutes I try to decipher whatever code it is I'm sure he's spelling out on my back. I focus hard. If he is communicating some secret message, however, it's DXYBCOZ. I decide he's just trying to confuse me. The back rubber is from L.A., where he organizes raves. He tells me he resents the popular perception that Burning Man is a hippie fest. "Hippies are just trying to relive the summer of sixty-three [sic]. We're here because we're artists. This is an artistic community."

My arms feel like they're being pulled out of their sockets by a computer programmer from Colorado who, like a large percentage of people at Burning Man, found out about the event over the Internet. "I was just surfing the Net and I kept hearing about this big party and it sounded so cool that I had to check it out for myself." He's come alone as, it turns out, have the other sunscreeners. I realize that this is what the Sunscreen Camp is all about. People who spend most of their days in front of a computer can drive a day or two, or however faraway Loneliness is, come to the Sunscreen Camp and talk to and touch real people.

Where Lonely People Gather

Of course this is true of Burning Man itself. People from around the country, and even from abroad, read about Burning Man on the Internet or find out about it from a *Wired* magazine article from the year before that seems to function as a *Let's Go* guidebook for a lot of these people coming to Burning Man, and simply by showing up and becoming participants can make friends with fifteen thousand people. People who will talk to them, massage them, give them drugs, dance with them.

Like the back rubber/rave organizer, the computer programmer views himself as taking part in an artists' republic. He massages my hands, and at one point locks fingers with me. "It's so important," he tells me while squeezing my hand, "for artists to connect."

I'm Not Sure Where I'm Going

As I'm leaving the Sunscreen Camp, a man on a bike with a cart trailing behind him rings the silver bell on his handlebar.

"Do you need a ride?" he asks.

"Sure," I say.

"Where do you need to go?"

There isn't anywhere in particular I need to go. But I've adopted the attitude that if I'm going to find Community I have to participate, experience, etc. I see a Canadian flag on the top of an RV in the distance and decide it's a reasonable ride from where we are to there and as good a place as any so I point toward it and say, "To Canada."

My chauffeur's name is Greg, he's about forty-five years old, and his bark-textured face is red and his eyebrows have been bleached white by the sun. This is Greg's fourth Burning Man. He's surprised when I ask him why he keeps coming back, as though there would be any reason why he *wouldn't* come back.

"The people here are great," he says, "and I love camping." I look around at the city of fifteen thousand cramped into the smallest possible quarters and think how this is more like refugee camping.

Before I get into the cart, Greg offers me a prize. I close my eyes and reach into a baseball cap that still feels sweaty around the rim and pull out a sticker that says, "Burning Man '97."

"Cool," I say, and get into the back of the cart where I sit on an upside-down milk crate. Before we take off Greg offers me a water bottle full of beer. The beer is murky and things are floating inside the water bottle so that it looks like an aquarium that hasn't been cleaned for a while.

"It's too hot to drink," I say. Even my desire to experience isn't enough to force me to stomach the concoction.

"Too hot to drink?" He makes a perplexed face and his blond eyebrows become one long mustache on his forehead and his wrinkles as pronounced as the lines of a [German engraver Albrecht] Dürer woodcut. He takes a swig, then another, and then a third really long one, and then we're off. We travel down the dirt road and pass by naked people on bikes—some dually disclothed on tandem bikes. The dirt rises and the wheels of the cart squeak and Greg pedals furiously. When we arrive at the Canadian flag he's out of breath. His face is redder, his eyebrows whiter.

I get off and thank him.

"Where are you going?"

"I'm not sure yet," I say.

"You mean you had me come all this way and it wasn't even your destination?"

I want to explain to Greg that because I don't know what I'm hoping to find or where, exactly, I think I might find it, I can't give him specific directions. But instead I shrug sheepishly.

"Well, have a good Burning Man," he says as he mounts his bike, looking like he's having second thoughts about liking *all* the people at Burning Man.

Burning Man Is Like the Internet

I make my way over to a camp that's called House of Doors, which is exactly that: at least forty doors of various shapes, sizes, and colors that have been hinged together. I walk by all the doors and look inside the area that's been created by the circumference of the doors, but there's no one there and not much to do except think, Where'd they get all these doors and how did they get them up here, and did they hinge together here or before they came? So I leave.

Next I go to Camp Boise. The people who set it up are from Idaho (judging by both the name of the camp and the Idaho license plates on their RV). You're supposed to visit these camps and "participate" in whatever's going on, so I sit down on a lawn chair in Camp Boise. But there's no one there—they're probably out checking out other people's camps who are out checking out other people's camps, etc. I wait for a while, nothing much happens, so I leave.

The more I walk around, the more I'm convinced that Burning Man is a physical manifestation of the Internet—essentially, it's a big open space that you can travel around however you choose. Considering that an impressive number of Burning Man-ners find out about the event on the Net or from *Wired* magazine, it makes sense that when given the tabula rasa of the desert, they use it to construct what they know best: real live Web sites. This insight begins to affect my perception of all the theme camps. When I run into people I've met in the line for Sunscreen Camp or hanging out at Cafe Temps Perdu and they ask me where I'm going, in my head I add domains to every response. "I'm going to the trojanhorse.edu" or "I'm headed toward icesculpture.com" or "I'm going to biancassmutshack.org."

Bianca's Smut Shack is supposed to be a house of ill repute, but no one's doing anything that could really give them a bad reputation; in fact, no one's doing much of anything. Bianca has hauled trucks full of ratty futons and mattresses and couches and positioned them under tarps. Everyone hangs out there looking artsy, bad, and heroin chic. It's as though the Smut Shack Slackers have seen too many ads for Diesel Jeans, the ads where it looks like the morning after a party (and at Burning Man, it always is the morning after a party) or that they're trying to be the alternative to the MTV Beach House. Instead of dancing around to music by swimming pools, they're sinking into Chianti-colored velveteen couches and occasionally painting each other's nails hues like jaundice.

Back at Our Camp, We Meet the Neighbors

In the early afternoon I make my way back to our campsite, orienteering myself by way of various Burning Man landmarks: I turn right at a big U-Haul that says "Come to Minnesota, land of 100,000 lakes," left at a trampoline, and right at a CNN RV. When I get back to our campsite Vanessa's sitting outside on one of our sun chairs in a bikini reading Freud's *Civilization and Its Discontents.* She's found a passage relevant to Burning Man and reads aloud, "Freud called it the contention that what we call our civilization is largely responsible for our misery, and that we should be much happier if we gave it up and returned to primitive conditions."

"What's interesting," she says, peering up at me over her sunglasses, "is that Freud could never check out his theories. I mean, imagine what he would have thought of Burning Man."

Before we can discuss this further, one of our neighbors, who has shoulder-length dark hair and perfectly even teeth, comes over and lurks near our table and chairs. Vanessa closes her thin paperback book with the definitiveness of someone closing a Bible, and we spend the rest of the afternoon getting to know our neighbors.

The word *neighbors* is an understatement because it implies that those camped around us live at a distance, when they're really in our face. The neighbor with the even teeth tells us, "I am a sponge. In real life, I'm an artist, but what I'm doing here is absorbing creativity."

He shows us a poem he once wrote and that he's had printed up on triangular-shaped business cards. He wrote it after he awoke from a coma eleven years ago. According to him, his girlfriend—she was a professional race car driver—tried to kill him because he didn't want to marry her. She took him on a fast ride, and because she was a professional, she managed to get him hurt when they crashed but she was unscathed.

"The reason I didn't want to marry her was because I got to know her and found out she wasn't a nice person," he tells us. "And of course, that feeling was confirmed when she tried to kill me."

Together with Coma Guy's camp, the four other camps bordering our campsite form a circumference about one yard away from us on all sides. Counterclockwise next to Coma Guy is Naked Man, who hangs out on his Pathfinder in the buff, but when it comes time to take a shower he goes behind a bamboo curtain.

Next to him and closest to my camp are three nineteen-year-old women from Oregon. They spend most of their time under a tentlike structure they've created by sewing together six tapestries and placing them over oval wires that look like gigantic croquet hoops. Under their tarp they literally navel gaze: They scrutinize their belly buttons, all of which are pierced. "I used to have a really pretty belly button," one of them says staring into her now-infected navel; for a moment she looks as though she might cry.

Next over are the musicians in the RV who have spent all their money to come to Burning Man. One is a vocalist who lives in Tucson and the other is a drummer from D.C. The guy from Tucson took on an extra job at an adult video store to pay for this year's event (the $800 RV rental, the $75 tickets, etc.). "There's a company in Sedona that I came into contact with through my job at the video store that would have paid me a thousand to come here this year and just shoot videos of all the naked women walking around here, but I couldn't do that because that would violate the anticonsumer environment of Burning Man," he tells me in complete earnestness. Upon spotting Vanessa's Freud he says, "Wow, doesn't that dude write about sex and stuff?"

My quietest neighbor is a plump, bespectacled computer programmer from Oregon. He drove twenty-four hours by himself to get here, he tells me with the *Wired* magazine article tucked under his arm, and he's looking forward to meeting people. I recommend he check out the Sunscreen Camp the next day.

What People Do at Burning Man

An unspoken schedule exists at Burning Man. At about dusk people go to their campsites to make dinner, change outfits, and put on makeup (here in Black Rock the men wear more than the women). As Vanessa and I sit outside our tent in our sun chairs and start off on the first two of our four total beers for the weekend, a twenty-year-old-looking boy with bright blue eyes and sun-kissed hair comes by and says, "How are you girls doing tonight?"

"Fine," Vanessa says.

"Do you need some Ecstasy?"

Although Burning Man is a consumer-free environment—nobody, including the organizers, is supposed to make a profit, and camps can't sell products, only "accept donations"—there's a tacit exception as far as drug sales are concerned.

We decline Blue-eyed Boy's offer and he stumbles off through the high grass to the next outside dining table. (He doesn't do RVs.) Coma Guy comes over and asks if we're doing any drugs.

"No," I tell him.

"Wow," he says. "Trippy."

The second it becomes dark, the parties begin. With them, the music starts getting louder and tiki torches suddenly abound as though it's the opening ceremony of the Olympics. We make our way to several parties—mostly raves, and to a party at a place called the Country Club, where everyone's dressed like white trash, drinking Schlitz beer and gorging themselves on family-size bags of potato chips. People at the parties do the same thing most people do at parties in Society—drink, smoke, dance—except that at Burning Man they're wearing less clothing. Walking around, I get the sense that a lot of people at Burning Man don't go to parties at home, and so a lot of them act the way they think people do at parties. People who don't go to a lot of parties must think that an orgy is a requirement of any crazy party because many participants use Burning Man as an excuse to have one. These are not the choreographed orgies of X-rated movies, but rather, awkward pile-ups of people who thrash around like nonswimmers dropped into the middle of a lake. The most common sites for the so-called orgies to take place are trampolines.

Some of the things we see as we walk around the streets and into camps: a man who lights himself on fire, and a woman with a fire extinguisher who puts him out; a man with a bag of Cheetos who walks around tossing his Cheetos at people saying, "Cheeto Man blesses you"; a woman whose entire body is painted green who serves Absinthe to whoever wants to pretend they're in a Hemingway story (or whoever just wants some); and a teenage girl who climbs up onto a gigantic rocking horse that must be about twenty feet high, looks out at the metropolis of Black Rock—at the lights and the dancing and the camps crowded all together, and the thousands of people—and yells, "Oh my God, it's a mad, mad world out there."

The History of Burning Man

On Saturday Vanessa and I go to check out the Man, close up. Although the effigy is ostensibly the raison d'être of the Burning Man community (not to mention its namesake) no one really pays it much attention. The Man's primary function is as a navigational tool; when people give directions they say "Our camp is to the Man's right," or "The concert will be at the Main Stage, which is directly behind the Man."

When we arrive there are only three other people visiting the Man, two women who are standing on the platform between his legs having their picture taken by a third. The pilgrimage to the Man is obviously not as mandatory as one would think. The Man is merely the outline of a man, a Calderesque figure you might draw when playing hangman. His head is like a Chinese lantern, he has no feet or hands, and the only modern aspect to his otherwise archaic construction is neon tubing: blue neon outlines his body; green emphasizes his bones, including his twelve ribs. During the day the neon is turned off, and I find something sad about this, like an unplugged Christmas tree.

As Vanessa and I stand on the platform underneath the Man I see that on the inside of his right leg, where his calf would be if he had one, is an iridescent 2-by-4 inch sticker depicting Jesus on the cross. This seemingly irreverent sticker doesn't surprise me; no one at Burning Man seems to be religious—if anything, they believe in the religion of New Ageness. The Burning Man festival is like a reverse Easter weekend—it's on Sunday that the protagonist of the Burning Man religion is destroyed rather than resurrected.

More than anyone else, Larry Harvey is the preacher to this community. Although two men were responsible for the original Burning Man in 1986, the other initiator, Jerry James, decided not to be a part of Burning Man this year after the disasters that occurred at Burning Man 1996. (Among the more tragic incidents, a car ran over a tent full of people.) So Harvey is now the sole leader of the event and its spokesperson. Harvey always sports his trademark Stetson hat, and people often say he looks as though he's the sheriff of a small town, which isn't fully accurate—he looks the way a sheriff of a small town would look in a Western movie. When he talks, he keeps the back of his jaw locked, as though he's chewing on a toothpick.

On Saturday afternoon Harvey gives a speech near the cafe. His "scheduled" topic is the history of Burning Man, and I attend hoping to have my questions about the significance of the Man answered. I want to ask Harvey about similarities between Burning Man and a description of the burning of a wicker man I'd come across in Caesar's *The Conquest of Gaul.*

But, I discover, everyone has their own interpretations of where Harvey must have gotten his idea from—everything from a movie called *The Wickerman* to Celtic harvest rituals are suggested as possible sources. Burning Man-ners even try to interpret Harvey's story—about how his girlfriend and he had split and he was at San Francisco's Baker Beach with some friends on the summer solstice and they decided to set fire to a man they had built out of lumber—to mean that the figure was a representation of the man his girlfriend left him for. But, Harvey maintains, there was no man she left him for; the figure represented his own human angst and it had nothing to do with her or the man. He was thirty-seven, going through a midlife crisis, and wanted something that would answer his questions about identity.

What the Founder Has to Say

Wearing black jeans, a blue button-up shirt, and, of course, his hat, Harvey stands in front of a banner that says "Save Burning Man." He smokes a cigarette, which he ashes into a half-crushed aluminum can and tells the story of the first time he set the man on fire. "The crowd instantly doubled as the figure ignited," Harvey says, pausing dramatically. "What we had created was a community. We did it again because it had created that community, and we never stopped to give it meaning. We never said, 'This is what it represents,' we never le;&.5qassigned a meaning to Burning Man because we were so invested in it that it didn't need to mean anything. Burning Man has always been about immediacy. From the start people organized around it in an informal but potent way."

The authorities got involved in 1989 when over three hundred people gathered to watch the man burn at Baker Beach, and the 1990 Burning Man was moved to Black Rock, in Washoe County, Nevada. This move to the desert is what led to what Harvey calls the "Modern Burning Man," to "an experiment in community." "It was a vast desert space, a great piece of nature. It was like water, but you could walk on it," Harvey says. "You had to make a commitment to getting here and to surviving in nature. In Society you work and get your pay and buy crap so you can work. Our culture here is based on communion, not consumption. We have re-created a culture."

People at Burning Man, Harvey says, "are rootless and looking for a community, and the only way we're going to get it is if we organize a community. Like a petri dish, a culture will grow in it," he says, in all seriousness, and then immediately follows this obviously rehearsed proverb with another: "We make the hive, you make the honey."

"Like a flower," he continues, evidently on a roll, "we spread contiguously. Not like franchises, but like dandelion seeds in the wind. We plan so that this spontaneous thing that you do will just happen."

In his book *The American Religion*, Harold Bloom writes about New Age religions: "You can sometimes construe a New Age passage and hazard some guess as to more or less what some California sage hoped she or he might mean. Otherwise, the student of the New Age must be resigned to that proverbial picnic, to which the authors bring the words (or some of them, anyway) and the readers bring the meanings."

Pop Psychology Meets Entrepreneurship

Larry Harvey certainly provides the proverbs, and is smart enough to let everyone else bring their meanings to Burning Man. He knows how desperate everyone is for it to mean *something*, but that no established meaning will suffice, especially for this crowd, who define themselves as being antirules, antisociety, and are therefore probably antirituals that have any specific significance. Harvey capitalizes on the crowd's antigovernment sentiments in his plea for money. Although the entrance fee to Burning Man more than doubled this year to $75, the operating deficit of Burning Man is $200,000 and the 1997 event costs $800,000. According to Marian Goodell, the Communications Mistress of Burning Man, the money goes to everything from Porta Potties, which cost $40,000, to the Man himself—the supplies for the Man cost $2,000; the neon, $3,000; the staff of twenty who work for two weekends before the event building the Man, almost $3,000. To satisfy safety concerns of Washoe County, Nevada commissioners, forty firefighters are on the scene at a cost of $258,000 to organizers, and it is Washoe County that Harvey rallies Burning Manners' antigovernment sentiments against. "We have been called locusts by the authorities of Washoe County," Harvey shouts. "We are not locusts but human beings. We need to work together."

Harvey is, of course, preaching to the converted. The crowd cheers; bike bells clink; a shirtless man wearing a straw hat and a shell necklace behind me yells out, "You can work with me, Larry."

Harvey asks everyone for a donation and says that if people give $500, they can come to Burning Man forever.

"Oh my God," the obviously stoned-out-of-his-mind guy with the shell necklace exclaims. The thought of coming to Burning Man forever is, at least at this moment, the most amazing thought to him, a dream come true.

Harvey concludes his incendiary sermon by saying, "Save Burning Man if you want to continue to see it live."

I leave without having had any of my questions about the significance of the ritual answered, but realizing that to hope for as much was to miss the point.

When I later pin down Harvey one on one, we have a long, circuitous conversation in which Harvey seems more human, less on his soap box, and more than a little overwhelmed by the cult status he has attained—people come to him for answers the way people once traveled to Lourdes for healing. I am no different. I ask him how he accounts for the fact that the figure of a man being burned shows up in so many different myths and cultures, why he thinks it touches something in our popular consciousness.

"There's a period in children's lives when they're in a state of identity formation, when they're trying to locate themselves and their place in the world and they begin drawing stick figures," Harvey says. "When you think about it, the man at Burning Man, in scale, is about how big we remember our parents when we were young. One of the ways we first realized we were ourselves was in relating to them. People relate to the figure of the Man because it is close to what they think they are. The figure of the man is our sense of individual identity made large."

If this is true, I ask Harvey, if he really believes the Man helps Burning Man-ners go through their own identity formation, how does he account for the fact that at the end of the weekend the Man is then set on fire. Again, Harvey turns to an analogy that involves a child's behavior. "The man is only useful as he enables us to go through a process. Once that process is over, we discard it as a child who, having gotten the experience he or she wanted, flings away a toy."

No One Is Sharing

On Sunday, I decide to get body-painted by Twinkle Fingers to show that I am, in fact, a participant. Twinkle Fingers is a masseur and body painter who is parked at an intersection by my tent. I've passed by him many times over the weekend and if I go elsewhere to get painted I'll feel like a traitor to my neighborhood. I've seen him at work with his fingers or else sleeping on his massage table, right there in the open, with one of those blindfolds they sometimes give you on airplanes over his eyes and nothing covering anything else.

"Twinkle Fingers, I presume," I say as I approach him. Hearing myself say those words I feel that maybe I have fallen through the looking glass.

"Yes?" he says.

I ask if he can do a little design on my shoulder and he sighs. "Okay," he says, less than enthusiastically, not the way you would think someone who calls himself Twinkle Fingers should say it.

Almost reluctantly, he takes out his aqua colors. Aqua colors come in little flat cylinders, like eye shadow, and Twinkle Fingers places them in a semicircle on the massage table next to where I'm sitting. Next, he backs away and stares at me as though I'm a blank canvas and he's waiting for his vision. Apparently, one comes to him because he says, "Okay, I'm ready," and he returns to the massage table. He sprays my skin with a water spritzer and then uses his fingers to spread the purple, turquoise, black, and silver paint on my skin. I can't see what he's doing but it feels like he's making a mess.

Twinkle Fingers is a little disappointed in Burning Man, he tells me, because he thought there would be more sharing. "I'm a masseur all year long—I travel around and work out of my van—and from what I read about this community everyone's supposed to bring something to share. So I brought my massage table and my paints, thinking that there would be a lot of free stuff going on. But no one else seems to be sharing."

I notice that he's using quite an excessive amount of the black paint and I wonder if this is an expression of his anger.

"Don't get me wrong," he continues, "I didn't come to Burning Man expecting anything in return, I'm just a little surprised is all."

Twinkle Fingers obviously feels guilty about his lack of altruism, but I now understand his initial hesitation to paint me. He feels he's being exploited, taken advantage of, and so in return I let him paint more of my body than I had originally planned—essentially my entire upper torso save the area covered by my bikini top. When he's done, he's concerned he may have relied a little too heavily on the black and to "brighten" me up he has me stand up and take a deep breath and close my eyes and then he sprays my entire torso with silver body glitter. For days after I return from Burning Man I continue to find flecks of the silver glitter on my clothes in my sleeping bag, in between my toes, and in my ears.

Conflict Arises

It turns out that Twinkle Fingers isn't the only one who's becoming disillusioned with Burning Man. As the day wears on, it becomes increasingly evident that the center is not holding.

I overhear a couple of fights about music among neighbors along the lines of "Would you please f--king stop afflicting us with your lack of taste in music," and I witness several altercations between bikers who, experiencing the Burning Man version of road rage, shout out, "Watch where you're going, asshole!" Near my camp, a guy's mountain bike is stolen. "That's so non-Burning Man," people around me say. "That's so not anticonsumerism."

"I think Freud was right," Vanessa says after we've been informed of the local bike theft. We're sitting outside our tent at our table and I'm using a wet rag to rub off some of what feels and looks like black lava on my skin. All I'm succeeding in doing is creating mud.

Vanessa continues, "Freud called into question the contention that civilization is largely responsible for our misery and that we would be much happier if we gave it up and returned to primitive conditions," she tells me, and pauses to hold up a gallon jug of water to her SPF 15 Chap Sticked lips and guzzle for a full minute.

"In fact, he found this contention 'astonishing,' because [she reads to me from a highlighted passage in the books], 'In whatever way we may define the concept of civilization, it is a certain fact that all the things with which we seek to protect ourselves against the threats that emanate from the sources of suffering are part of that very civilization.'"

Our rocker neighbors come over ostensibly to admire my body art, but really only because there are no barriers telling them they can't just come over and interrupt us whenever they want.

The Grrrlie Grrrl Room

Despite the increasing disgruntlement, or maybe because of it, Sunday is the most participatory day of all. Too participatory it turns out: When Vanessa goes to the Sunscreen Camp to get lotioned up, she's told that one of the volunteers was asked to leave because more than a few women complained that he was too liberal with his sunscreen application and "put sunscreen where the sun doesn't go."

One of the main attractions on Sunday is a new camp opening at 2:00 P.M. called the Grrrlie Grrrl Room. At first I think the "grrr" spelling is derived from Riot Grrrls, punk rock girls who felt they were being ignored by the music scene in the eighties and to show their anger—their grrr—started writing 'zines. But the "grrr" of the Grrrlie Grrrl Room, I discover, seems far removed from anger, and if anything is evocative of the sounds of the camp's ample supply of sex devices, or else the sounds that are emitted upon use of the aforementioned supplies. The Grrrlie Grrrl Room is a group masturbation room for women in honor of this year's Burning Man theme—fertility—as though any camp at Burning Man needs an excuse, like a theme, to revolve around sex. The entrance is a red fur-lined, female genital-shaped opening with a white sheet hanging down behind it for privacy. Inside the room leopard skin fabrics are draped over beds, wicker chairs, and on the ground. There's pornography to read and appliances to use. Safe sex is even a consideration: Condoms are supplied, as are plastic Ziploc baggies for the "larger-than-life" dildos. Soft Enya-esque background music floats through the room. It's an all-women crowd for the hour between two and three, and when a woman is about to achieve her goal, she is cheered on by the others. "You go, girl," a chorus chants, and after, applauds.

At 3:00 P.M. males are allowed in the Grrrlie Grrrl room, but only with a female hostess, and I suddenly have many male friends—people I've met over the past few days who want to see what the Grrrlie Grrrl Room is about and view me as their ticket in. A reporter I've met at Burning Man tries to convince me to escort him in, but fails. Instead, I head toward Crazy Dante's Used Soul Emporium.

Having My Soul Appraised

The way the Soul Emporium works is that you fill out a questionnaire designed to appraise your soul and then a sales representative evaluates how many points your soul is worth, and depending on how many points you have, you can exchange your soul for Arsenio Hall's or Hugh Grant's or whoever else at Burning Man has already traded theirs in." . . . Often, you have to barter your way for a soul and try to argue why you deserve someone else's soul, even if you don't have enough points.

I sit down to answer the questionnaire, which ends up taking me a while because the questions are tough so I start with the easiest first. Question #2: *Describe the last request you absolutely refused to fulfill.* I respond: "Taking a man into the Grrrlie Grrrl Camp." The other questions force me to write down things I've done that I regret, how many people I've slept with (and if I wish the number were higher or lower), and to list any lies I've ever told. I've never before had to evaluate my life with such honesty and I can't believe it takes a Burning Man theme camp to make me do so.

When I'm finally ready to have my Soul Appraisal Questionnaire evaluated by a Personal Sales Representative, I'm told that the Used Soul Emporium is closing down for a couple of hours (even the Emporium is slacking in the participation department). So I put my questionnaire in my shorts pocket and plan on coming back. Shortly after I leave the Emporium I take the questionnaire out and unfold it to make sure my name's not on it, just in case it should fall out and into the wrong hands. It's not, so I fold it back up and restuff it in my pocket.

What It All Means

There's a general feeling of anticipation for the remainder of the afternoon. People are anxious for nine o'clock, when the Man is going to be set on fire. In the meantime the thought of fifteen thousand people making a grand exodus the following morning is enough to send more than a few campers packing their cars and RVs so they can make a quick getaway as soon as the Man burns.

It's the last day of Burning Man, and I'm still not sure What It All Means. Still feeling slightly cheated by the Soul Emporium, I compose my own mental questionnaire and I pass the afternoon talking to my neighbors about what the burning of the man means to them.

Sprawled on the ground near my tent talking to Coma Guy is Shawn. Stout and pallid, Shawn is wearing camouflage pants and a plaid shirt. He's focused on spinning one of the foot pedals of his Mongoose mountain bike, which is resting beside him. It turns out he knows Coma Guy from Burning Man last year. They kept up their friendship because after

Burning Man each year there are Burning Man parties in warehouses in San Francisco. It's not uncommon for five hundred people to show up at these parties (they find out about it through the Internet, of course) and show their Burning Man slides (while drinking, drugging, and dancing) and talk about how great last year's Burning Man was, and how great next year's will be.

Shawn has a definite idea of what the burning of the man means: "Mankind f--ks everything up, so by burning the man you're saying f--k you to society and saving the Earth." He gives the pedal of his bicycle a whirl, looks up at me and adds, "But I guess that's a pretty cliché view of it."

Another man I talk to who is in his fifties and on a bike tells me that he saves up all his anger every year and when the Man burns, his inflammatory rage turns to ashes. He's smiling while he's telling me this, and I can't help thinking that he looks like the most peaceful person at Burning Man. I tell him this, and he smiles even wider and says, "Well, it's my fifth year coming here," as though that explains everything.

The nineteen-year-old neighbor women are under their homemade tent once again. Two apply sunscreen to each other's skin—something they've been doing all weekend although they rarely emerge from the tent except at night. The third goes through an entire box of baby wipes while removing the blue body paint she was covered head to toe in the night before at a rave.

The blue girl has dyed blond hair and tells me that she came the year before hoping that she would figure out what the hell the Burning Man meant. "But I realize that the reason it works as a symbol is the same reason a poem or a book or a piece of art can be so stimulating. Everyone can interpret it how they want."

The girl who once upon a time had a pretty navel joins in. "Yeah, I think the older something is, the more people feel that they have to give a meaning to it. It could have been totally random."

My vocalist neighbor, who has now painted his face like some hard core Norwegian band he idolizes, shows me a video of the Daughters of Ishatar opera that took place the night before on the *playa* (the vast area beyond the campsites—the "wilderness" beyond Black Rock City). The opera ended, of course, with a big fire, which he has on tape, too. He's going to make a documentary out of the opera footage and send it to all his neighbors at Burning Man, he tells me. He's glad he taped it because he won't be able to tape it next year.

"Why not?" I ask.

"I'm going to have to sell the camera to pay for next year's trip to Burning Man."

His friend, the drummer, comes over and gives me one of his CDs. I ask him what the burning of the man will mean to him.

"It will mean it's time to go home," he says.

Fifteen Thousand Strong, We Walk Toward the Man

At seven o'clock the Society Cocktail Party begins in the center of camp. The outfits are more outrageous than usual, the stilts taller, and the drinks stronger. Even my sister seems to have undergone a conversion; in lieu of her Banana Republic halter top, she's sporting a green lei, and in her right hand is a gin and tonic. Fifteen thousand people is a lot—you see this when you look at Burning Man from the outside and mistake it for a budding metropolis—but by Sunday night's cocktail party I realize I either know or recognize a fair number of the attendees. I even run into some guys I went to high school with who are dressed as bunnies. Pink bunny suits—complete with painted-on whiskers and cottonball tails—have been their standard outfit every year they've come to Burning Man, but they wear them only on the final night, tonight, the night of the Burn. Upon spotting them, friends they've made from Burns past shout out, "Hey, it's the bunnies!" It almost feels like . . . a community.

At eight o'clock drums begin to drown out the rest of the music that's being played—even the techno music is at last defeated—and tiki torches are lit. A crowd stands around the fire pit where, for the first time this year, a solar-induced fire was started. One of the rangers explains to me that this fire is like "the eternal flame at the Olympics."

"Oh really?" I say. "How long has it been going for?"

"Since Wednesday."

"Oh."

"It's a new ritual this year," he tells me. "That's the great thing about Burning Man. I mean, look around, new rituals are being made up all the time."

Torches are lit by the fire of the fire pit, and soon I find myself in a procession of fifteen thousand people walking and dancing and chanting and drumming down the long street that leads to the figure of the Man. The Man alternates between flashing just his twelve green ribs and then his full blue and green colors.

Something amazing happens as fifteen thousand people make their way toward the Man. Both his arms, which have been by his side all weekend long, rise up at the same time. They keep rising up until they are above his lantern head. The crowd goes even crazier if this is possible, the drums get even louder, and the chanting becomes contagious, like a song you can't get out of your head, and suddenly I find myself singing, too.

In my dash to the front of the crowd, I've become separated from my sister and my bunny friends. I look around for them and instead see waving rubber chickens and cows and swans, Burning Man versions of animals to be sacrificed.

People start yelling, "Burn the Man!" and one guy walks around with an electronic display that flashes red letters that say "Burn!" The fire marshals and the Burning Man Project volunteers miraculously stop the crowd from getting too close and manage to make everyone form a gigantic semicircle around the Man, at a distance of about thirty feet back from him. I know this because I'm up front.

Meeting Secret

Suddenly, a guy in shorts and dyed blond hair runs from the base of the man, ducking fire patrollers and slides in next to me like a baseball player sliding into home. His name is Secret, he tells me, when he catches his breath.

"Why are you called Secret?" I ask.

"I can't tell you," he says.

Secret is good-looking in a *Dawson's Creek* kind of way. In a non–*Dawson's Creek* way, he's wearing black eyeliner beneath his wide eyes and an attached set of five eight-inch-long nails on his right hand. The claw has batteries and is lit up a glow-in-the-dark red. I tap one of the red fingers the way you tap an iron, expecting it to be hot, but it's not.

"Cool," I say.

"I hate that man," he tells me.

For a moment, I think he's talking about someone sitting near us, but then I see that he's staring at the forty-foot Man. The neon from the effigy lights up Secret's eyes and they do, in fact, look like angry eyes.

"Why do you hate him?"

"Why? Because he represents everything I'm angry about."

"What are you angry about?"

"Society. Corporate America. The media." He turns his angelic face to me and says, "What are you angry about?"

"Me? Nothing." I feel like a Spectator.

We talk a little more and Secret tells me he is twenty-one and from a small town outside of Sacramento. He heard about Burning Man from all the raves he goes to in San Francisco, and this is his third year coming back. He thinks they should have Burning Man twice a year because once a year isn't enough.

"Are you sacrificing anything to the Man?" he says.

"What?"

"Did you put anything underneath the man?" he says.

It occurs to me that this is what he was doing before he sprinted past the fire marshals and dove in beside me.

"No," I say. "What are you sacrificing?"

"Pizza."

"Large or small or a slice?" I ask.

"A large box."

"Pepperoni?"

"No," Secret tells me. "It was just the box."

"Just the box?" I say.

"Yeah."

"Why?"

"Because I work for Godfather's Pizza and I hate my job. I'm sacrificing that box so that with it I can Burn all my anger."

"Corporate America," I say.

"Yeah," he says. "You understand." He looks at me lovingly, this angry boy, and then he takes his red claw and massages my now dirt-and-dry-heat dread-locked hair with them. It feels good and I'm enjoying this weird Freddy Kruger version of a head massage and I'm feeling very relaxed until someone behind us yells, "Burn him."

And then it happens.

The Moment Arrives

A man is set on fire. Not the man you're thinking of, but a real man is set on fire in between the Burning Man's legs. Eventually he is extinguished, and the Burning Man himself is ignited with the help of diesel (past years have proven gasoline to be too volatile). He starts to burn simultaneously at the end of each limb.

Everyone is cheering or drumming and going wild. The fire races up the Man's legs, more quickly up his left; and down his arms, more quickly down his right. Catching fire, the neon tubes start emitting a sizzling sound, not unlike the sound of three million mosquitoes being simultaneously zapped.

The burning goes on for forty-five minutes; I'm so mesmerized it seems like only two. The sky is lit orange from the glow, and so are everyone's faces around me. When the entire frame of the Man has finally been weakened, he falls forward a little, as though he's received a hard punch in the stomach, and then he starts to fall back. It is the most alive the Man has seemed, his body moving as though his joints can rotate. He finally falls to his left, and then to the ground with a crash and sparks.

Fifteen thousand people scream. Everyone around me jumps up, as though to assert their triumph: The man has fallen and they are standing. The entire night sky looks like it's been eclipsed by the sun, and there is a flame where there once was a man, and orange sparks shoot up into the sky and out like fireworks. Some spiraling-downward sizzling sparks land on my arm and burn, proof that I am really here.

I find myself jumping up and down with adrenaline and the beauty of a lit sky in a wide desert. For the first time, I truly feel a part of this community and suddenly I understand the strange beauty of this even stranger ritual. On the verge of being knocked over by the chaos and excitement of it all, I grab onto something to steady me. I'm holding on for I don't know how long when I realize that I've locked fingers with Secret's glowing claw.

"Let's dance around it," Secret says, and pulls my hand with his claws. Secret is a veteran Burning Man-ner and my Virgil to the Inferno-esque ritual. He knows that once the man falls, everyone dances around him, one time, two times, all night.

Not Quite What I Expected

I'm still (and even more inexplicably since I'm now conscious of it) holding tight onto his red claw when he asks me if I've heard of Herakleitos. At first I think he must be talking about a rave in San Francisco (he's already told me that he's heard the rave scene in New York is beat and feels bad for me that I don't live near the good raves, i.e., the ones in San Francisco). But it turns out he is, in fact, talking about the Greek philosopher.

"Herakleitos is the man!" Secret says. "Have you read what he's said about fire? He says it's passion and everything around us. That's what Burning Man is all about, that's what this fire is all about. It's all about passion."

Having incited passion, Secret leans over, and holding the small of my back with his claw, he kisses me. I feel myself pulling away, I hear myself telling him I have a boyfriend.

"Did you know that Larry Harvey first burned the Man to represent the guy his girlfriend left him for?" Secret says.

I want to explain to Secret that this isn't quite the case, but it's what Secret chooses to believe (along with the idea that the Man represents society, corporate America, the media, et al.) so I nod. He lets me go and holds up his red claw as though to assure me, Okay, claw off. It's awkward between us—isn't separation always that way?—and I look around for an exit from the situation. What's transpired is the opposite of what's supposed to happen when a couple kisses in movies—the Kiss after which the music swells, the colors brighten, and everything in the world is right because Love has been found.

Instead, I feel ill.

The Significance of Ritual

I feel alone, so *not* a part of any community that there must be a word for it—*de*communitized—and something else. The sense that rather than having had an epiphany about Burning Man, what I was really experiencing was a moment of temporary insanity. I was caught up in the moment, the fifteen thousand people, the fire. I was caught up, so desperately, in the desire for it to mean something, for it all to mean something.

I think back on what Larry Harvey said to me, that the Man is only useful as he enables us to go through a process of identity formation and that once that process is over, we discard it as a child who, having gotten the experience he or she wanted, flings away a toy. Is this the case with all rituals, I wonder?

Of course, Burning Man is different from other rituals I've focused on because it's not exclusive to young women. But, like many of the initiations young women go through today, Burning Man is about having an identity within a community, about having a place in the world. After spending the long weekend trying to make the metamorphosis from spectator to participant, and observing others do the same, and then watching the Man, the figure people have travelled from around the world to be united by, burn to ashes, I can't help thinking, What happens after young women go through the ritual that they think will make them belong? What next?

In the distance I spot my sister and our bunny friends and when I catch up to them, we take a walk on the *playa*. The night is warm and the sky is the color of autumnal leaves. We go to glow-in-the-dark discos, and to parties, and to concerts, and watch women spinning tiki torches around with the same hand motions they'd use to jump rope.

The Continuing Search

We go to a camp called Circus X and watch topless women twirling batons. Topless women have been twirling batons all weekend long whether at the circus or not and the crowd becomes restless. "Burn it!" someone yells, and other incendiaries join in to form a chorus. It's not clear what they want to have burned. Just something. *Anything*. It's gotten to the point where fire is the only show people want to watch. Nearby, an objet d'art is torched and everyone abandons the circus for the flames.

In the dark and because it is on fire, it's difficult to make out exactly what is being burned, but I'm fairly certain it's the wooden Trojan Horse sculpture I've passed by several times. The fire is as big as a tall, fat tree, and suddenly there are a hundred naked and clothed people crowded around it.

We roam like nomads from one fire to another, and soon find ourselves lost. With no Burning Man at the center of the city, it's difficult to determine one's position in the camp. To further complicate matters, cars and vans have already started leaving, so landmarks like buses and U-Hauls—once our signposts in this makeshift community—have left only dirt where once there was direction.

Others, it seems, are not as lost, for when Vanessa and I say goodbye to the bunnies and travel toward where we think we'll find our car, we see approximately fifty people gathered around a bright white light. The image reminds me of a photograph I once saw of winter-parka-bundled people huddled around a light at the North Pole, trying to catch a bit of artificial sunlight in the dark days of winter.

But this light is different. It's just a white light in the middle of the desert that slowly spins like a barber's pole. Amazed, Vanessa and I continue to watch as it becomes later and later, and not one of the fifty observers moves: they all lay on their stomachs, some staring straight at the light, others observing it through the lens of their videocameras. At first we find this amusing, even laughable—all these video cameras will come back from Burning Man with hours of footage of a white light going around and around in circles.

But later, once we have found our car and miraculously made our way out of the ghost town that Black Rock City has become and onto the highway, I'm driving on into the dark, into nowhere, in silence because Vanessa's sleeping in the passenger seat, and I find myself surprisingly saddened by the image. All these people who want so desperately to be a part of a community, to have their identity defined by that community, that even when the ritual that has brought them together is over, when its central signifier has literally been burned to the ground, they search for something else, for anything—even if it's merely a white light—around which they can gather together again.

Jonestown: Not the Paradise I Thought It Would Be

Deborah Layton

In 1978, nearly one thousand men, women, and children died in a mass suicide orchestrated by Jim Jones, the pastor of the cult known as the Peoples Temple. Many of the cult's members had moved to Jonestown, located in Guyana in South America in the mid-1970s with the promise of living in a modern-day Eden. However, after their arrival they soon became enslaved to grueling agricultural work in the middle of the jungle with little more to eat than rice and beans. Jones envisioned his commune as a world free from the persecution of the government. Instead, as Deborah Layton's memoir reveals, it was a hostile and violent environment dictated by the inhumane and paranoid tactics of a tyrant. In this excerpt, Layton describes many of the injustices and hardships that she observed while living in isolation in the jungles of South America, especially the fake suicide ritual Jones practiced with his members, known as White Nights, in which they were made to drink Kool-Aid that had purportedly been laced with cyanide. In this excerpt, Layton reveals how even her own mother, who joined the Peoples Temple and who became ill during her stay at Jonestown, was subjected to Jones's cruelty.

It had been several weeks since our arrival and by now I was accustomed to the unusual smells in the food and drink. I was even unaffected by the rice weevils and other strange bugs we ingested daily. Now I, too, ate enormous mounds of rice covered in gravy.

Christmas had come and gone without fanfare and I had acclimated to this new life of physical labor and late night ag-

Deborah Layton, *Seductive Poison: A Jonestown Survivor's Story of Life and Death in the Peoples Temple*, New York, NY: Doubleday, 1998.

ricultural meetings. I knew I had been here for at least three weeks because I had taken and passed three socialism tests.

In spite of our isolation in the jungle, we knew everything that was happening all over the world because Father [Jim Jones] read us newspaper and magazine articles over the loudspeakers daily. He told us in detail how violent the United States had become and how his place in history, as a great leader, was being tarnished by the evil defectors in America. Whenever he read to us about the vicious actions being taken by our government against innocent people, I was relieved we lived here. I learned of a leader in Uganda named Idi Amin, who apparently was a great diplomat. Father said we should learn to emulate his "wild actions." He said that when people acted like "crazy niggers," the establishment would back off and leave them alone. He said this was how we would begin to act here, too. If we threatened various government agencies with killing ourselves or leaving the country in a mass exodus, we would get our way more easily. Everything, he said, was done for effect. He had to test how far he could and should push them. It never occurred to me that these tests one day would turn into ghastly reality.

I still worked the fields but had been reassigned to Lorina's crew as Lee had been pulled from the fields to oversee the construction of more housing. Father had announced an incentive program: On Sundays, the only day we had the late afternoon free, those people who wanted a relationship and had gone through the approval process, could begin to construct their own cabins. Within hours, the relationship list quadrupled. Mark came to me that same day and asked if I would like to live with him, but I had decided on my first day that I would not pursue this dangerous course. My excuse to him was that the Cause was more important to me than an egocentric relationship and, anyway, he was hardly ever in Jonestown. Although he had helped prepare the land and original buildings for our arrival, he was now becoming a licensed ship captain at Father's behest. Father had decided that we needed to purchase a larger boat for our next emigration, to a more friendly country. The Six-Day Siege had deeply affected and deformed his perception of our safety and there were discussions of our moving to Cuba or the Soviet Union. On a couple of occasions, when I visited the radio room to ask Carolyn a question, I overheard small talk about visiting the embassies of socialist countries in the capital. Mark seemed discouraged, and it was hard to let go of such an old dream, but my decision was made. . . .

Life was tough in the Promised Land. The physical labor during the day was grueling but it was nothing compared to the terror we experienced at night. Every night, someone was confronted. Every night, I was afraid I, or someone I was close to, would be next.

Tortured by His Own Son

During one emergency meeting I was perched in my customary place near Jim's son Stephan, biting deeply into my cheek to stay awake, when I felt my head jerking backward.

Had the guards seen me? I began to breathe in slowly and deeply, and started my self-preservation mantra: Look alert! Stay awake! I bit harder, drawing blood, fighting sleep, fighting to keep my body erect. I knew how dangerous it was to be found inattentive or sleepy, but it was getting harder every night.

From somewhere in the crowded Pavilion came a rustling sound. Oh no! I thought. Someone's fallen from the bench. Someone's fallen asleep!

"Stand!" Father bellowed over the loudspeaker. "Are you not afraid? Do *you* believe that *you* are different from the rest of us? Speak up and explain yourself," he hissed.

Charlie, a sixty-year-old father of five, stood up, brushing the dirt from his pants. "Father, I'm sorry. I did not mean to—" He was cut off by shouting. Everyone was angry. Someone always had to do this. Now Jim was furious, and we were going to have to confront Charlie and everything would drag on even longer. But no wonder Father was mad. If we were attacked now, Charlie would be our weak link. We must be careful, ever watchful of the weak one. Falling asleep proved that your head was in the wrong place, which made you more susceptible to committing treason.

"So, you think falling asleep during an emergency meeting is easy? Let's see how you fare with this. Put the snake around his neck!" One of the guards carried a ten-foot boa constrictor's cage into the middle of the Pavilion and opened the door.

"No! Wait," Father yelled. "Get Charlie's son to do it. I want Nick to put the snake around his daddy's neck."

There was a chilled silence. Nick was one of the most trusted and well-like guards in the camp. Was Jim testing his loyalty?

"Oh God, please, Father, *no*! No, don't!" Charlie begged as Nick devoutly weighed his Father down with the massive serpent.

"Jim, please. It's just that the field work is—"

"Stop your sniveling," Father demanded.

"Shut up, man! You're an embarrassment," Nick muttered.

"What's that?" Father asked. "You ain't crying about this, are you, Nick?"

"Hell no, Father." Nick wiped at his eye. "The f---g snake's tongue scratched my cornea," he lied.

Jim chuckled into the microphone. "Why are all of you so quiet out there? Where's your indignation? I want you to scream out why you hate Charlie! Anyone too prissy to scream will find themselves up here with this snake when I'm done with Chuckie-boy."

"Why don't we put him in the Box, Father?" a frail voice from somewhere in the Pavilion called out.

"'Cause we got Jeff in there. And he ain't comin' out for a while." Father looked around. "Who the hell asked that stupid question? Stand! Was you sleepin' in our last meetin' when Jeff was dragged off to the Box?"

"No, Father. I just thought maybe he'd been taken out by now," said the voice, becoming weaker with fear.

"What do I hear in your voice? Sorrow? Do you feel sorry for Jeff? He's an antirevolutionary. He'd turn on you in a second if the mercenaries came in right now. He's being punished for his refusal to stop daydreaming. Don't you remember?"

Suddenly there was nervous laughter near Father. A puddle was forming around Charlie and his pants were wet. Father's attention was successfully drawn away from another confrontation.

"Okay! Get the snake off him. His face is getting red." There was quiet commotion as three guards struggled to remove the constricting snake from Charlie's puffy neck.

"Now, let this be a warning to all of you," Father growled. "You will all be tested again and again, whether it be watching to see if you are working hard in the fields or by sending one of my spies out to pretend they want to leave. You better report them! 'Cause if you don't, you'll be up here, too, with a boa hanging from your neck and begging me for my forgiveness. That's right, even your son or daughter will be doing my bidding by testing your loyalty to the Cause. Don't let me down. Report the traitors to Carolyn or me."

I Had to Be on Guard at All Times

My head jerked again and I was suddenly aware that Stephan was sitting close enough to me to keep me from falling sideways and Lew, another of Jim's sons, was behind me with his hand on my back, both of them ensuring that I wasn't next. I realized how lucky I was, and shuddered at the thought of being punished. The Learning Crew seemed bad enough, but I didn't know how I would survive the Box.

The Box was a small underground cubicle to which even children would be sentenced if they had thought or done something Father thought punishable. It was six by four feet, dark, hot, and claustrophobic. Poor Jeff had been kept inside for ten days. People kept there were given nothing but mush to eat and drink. There was also the Well, a punishment used especially for children. They would be taken to the Well in the dark of night, hung upside down by a rope around their ankles, and dunked into the water again and again while someone hidden inside the Well grabbed at them to scare them. The sins deserving such punishment included stealing food from the kitchen, expressing homesickness, failing a socialism exam, or even natural childish rebelliousness. Their screams were chilling but we had learned from the consequences of previous people's objections not to complain.

People who could not be reeducated and continued to voice unhappiness or dissatisfaction were put in the Medical Unit. There, they were involuntarily drugged into acquiescence and maintained in that state indefinitely. These punishments effectively silenced all outward dissent. I consoled myself by remembering that these punishments were nothing compared to being captured by the enemy and tortured to death.

Thankfully, I kept a good rapport with most people around me, with the guards and my crew, and I had the quiet protection of Lee, Stephan, and Lew. I stood in for [Maria] in the radio room one morning while waiting for my work crew to assemble. While she ran to the loo, I operated the radio, feeling quite confident in my repartee with Paula in the capital. I had heard and seen Teresa do enough of it to know the call signs and a few codes. After this, Maria occasionally asked me to stand in for her while she ran down and talked to Jim at their house. For some reason she seemed to feel less threatened, or perhaps less jealous, of me now that I labored in the fields like everyone else. I had begun to drop a lot of weight, my pants were baggy, my hands had calluses and blisters, and my boots were almost worn out. Maria seemed concerned about me. She even became conciliatory and always brought me meat or a hard-boiled egg from Jim's personal fridge as a gift. I hoped she would tell Father who was holding down the fort while they discussed business.

Experiencing a White Night

One evening after my seventh socialism exam, I was beckoned over to the radio room by Carolyn. Maria was packing up her day communications notepads and talking to Jim. When she saw me, she smiled. I noticed that she had lost more weight.

"Grace will cause a siege . . ." Jim moaned, rubbing his hands together and looking sallow. Father usually stayed in the radio room all night with Carolyn, giving orders to Teresa in the States. Carolyn stepped outside the room and invited me to sit on the step with her.

"Debbie, I may need your help tonight," she said. "Annie has caught the bug that is going around. She may be too sick to care for John-John and Kimo for a while. Trouble's brewing . . . Jim's been anxious and unable to sleep for several days now."

"But I hear him—"

"Sshhh . . ." Carolyn put her finger to her mouth. "Tapes . . . He decides which ones should be replayed." She sighed. "He's taken ill, too, and during the day he rests, trying to catch up on his strength before another all-night session in here. He gets a lot of severe headaches and has a skin inflammation that needs medical attention."

I turned toward Jim, who was giving instructions to the States.

"Make sure the Concerned Relatives are watched," he yelled into the mike. "The Mertles, the Stoens, and every other SOB.

Tail them and find out who they're in contact with! This could be the end if they start writing letters to their congressmen."

Carolyn must have noticed my puzzled face.

"The traitors have begun an organization called Concerned Relatives," she explained to me. "They are trying to organize families concerned about their kids to join forces against us . . ." She lowered her voice. "Listen, just go to your cabin and try to sleep. There may be trouble later."

I obediently went to my cabin, kicked off my filthy work pants, covered my head with my pillow, and instantly fell asleep.

Late that night, in the midst of my heavy sleep, sirens began to blare. I heard guards banging on cabin doors and yelling. Frightened and disoriented, I sat up.

"Security alert! Hurry, everyone! Anyone late will be punished."

I wondered if this was what Carolyn had alluded to. My heart was racing. I jumped down from my bunk. Father's voice was screaming over the P.A. system.

"Danger! Security alert! Hurry, everyone. Danger is near!"

Sick with fear I tried to remember what I had done with my pants. They weren't on my bed or my trunk.

"White Night!" Father yelled over the loudspeaker.

My roommates were already out the door. I was on my belly, groping for my boots and pants, frantic that someone had taken them as a joke. Finally I found them, pulled them on, bolted out the door, and bumped into one of the guards.

"Wow," he blurted out. "Sorry, Deb. This is your first . . . You better hurry, you're late. I'd hate you getting on the Learning Crew."

I wondered if I had time to use the bathroom. I knew I couldn't wait. Jogging toward the bright lights of the Pavilion,

Jim's voice shrieking orders, I veered off toward the showers and relieved myself standing. Residents rushed by, children were crying.

I heard gunfire in the forest. I ran to the radio room as Carolyn had told me to do earlier that evening, and waited for further instructions. Everyone had gathered in the Pavilion. I could see Mama [the author's mother], white as a sheet, seated directly in front of Jim.

"Darlings, we are under attack." Father looked wired, the way I had in high school when I was on speed.

"Remember those murderous family members we have chosen to leave and forget? They have formed a vicious group called the Concerned Relatives. The CIA has joined forces with them. We are under siege. The United States Government does not want us to survive. They threaten to surround, attack, torture, and imprison us. We don't want that, do we?"

Suddenly the air was filled with a frightening noise. A screaming and trilling sound, made by all the residents of Jonestown flicking their tongues, resonated through the jungle. I imagined the sound could be heard for miles, perhaps all the way to Port Kaituma. They must think we're mad, I thought.

"Louder! Let the mercenaries hear us," Father hissed into the mike and then joined in.

I wanted to run away, but stayed at the radio room awaiting my instructions from Carolyn. The encampment's security force marched around the Pavilion, counting to make sure each resident was present, checking every building to confirm, for our own safety, that everyone was there and attentive, in order to reinforce our commitment to be good disciples.

Maria was on the radio trying to make herself heard through the ferocious screaming in the Pavilion. After a while, Carolyn came to the stairs and told me everything would be fine.

"I forgot that this is your first White Night," she murmured softly. "Go sit with Stephan on the fence."

I anxiously climbed the four-foot wooden railing and positioned myself next to him, hoping I hadn't called any unnecessary attention to myself. We were some fifteen feet from Jim's chair. My hands were shaking, I began to bite the inside of my lip to stay focused. Adrenaline was pulsing through my body, but my exhaustion was equally great and I could feel myself losing and then regaining consciousness. I bit harder. We listened to the droning sound of Father's voice, an endless harangue in which he prophesied that we would be killed by our enemies.

He Told Us the End Had Come

I wondered why he didn't know what Carolyn knew, that everything was fine, that the peril had passed. But Father continued in a hysterical state, yelling over the loudspeaker, "All is lost. Traitors have betrayed us. Because of their disloyalty, their capitalistic self-indulgence, you, my good followers, have been condemned to death. Because of them and what they have said about us, we must die."

A mother spoke from the microphone situated at the middle of the Pavilion. I could tell from her voice that she had experienced this before.

"But the children, Father. Can't they at least live?"

"Darling, my darling . . ." Father's voice was sweet, consoling, and filled with misery. Tears had begun to streak his cheeks. "But who would care for our children, once we are dead? The enemy won't. Did you hear me tonight? They will take our babies and torture them. Have you forgotten our Six-Day Siege? How close they came to invading our sovereign territory?"

Then he cried aloud, "There is no way out, no resolution, my dear mother. Our enemies have outnumbered us."

There was more gunfire in the jungle. The mother moved back to her place on a bench, hugging her sleeping infant to her breast. I looked around for Carolyn. I must tell her, I thought, that she is mistaken. It was almost dawn. The night sky had lightened to a soft metallic blue and I realized that we had been here for at least six hours.

"Hear that sound?" Jim asked us. "The mercenaries are coming. The end has come. Time is up. Children . . . line up into two queues, one on either side of me."

Guards had placed a large aluminum vat in the front of the Pavilion near Father.

"It tastes like fruit juice, children. It will not be hard to swallow . . ."

I jumped down from the fence to stand in line with the others. I was confused and scared and didn't understand what was happening. Who were these people coming in to kill us?

A young man's voice yelled out in protest. "No! I don't want to die. There must be another way . . ."

"Guards! Take him and secure him. He'll have to be given the drink by force."

I looked around for Carolyn and saw her rushing from the radio room, her eyes filled with terror as she passed me, her face flushed as she approached the podium and began to whisper to Father. Father stopped his tirade to listen.

I could hear Stephan muttering something from under his breath. He turned to me, his eyes filled with contempt.

"The f---ing bastard," he gasped. "It's another bloody drill, that's all. Another f---g scare tactic . . ." He shook his head, exhausted.

"The crisis has been quelled," Father yelled into the loudspeaker. "The crisis is over. You may go back to your cabins. We will have a day of rest today. Yes. Kitchen staff, make a treat for our comrades. Let us have Sunday cookies tonight."

Alarmed, I glanced about for Mama, but did not see her. I wondered why Stephan had called his father a bastard? I remembered that Jim had sent him here before the other boys because he felt that Stephan was becoming disrespectful and might leave. . . .

Alarmed and filled with dread, I headed to my cabin. I felt dizzy and my head was aching. Why had Father persisted in talking about an attack when Carolyn had told me all was fine? Why had Carolyn waited so long before talking to Father to quiet his hysteria? Why had I heard gunfire? What in God's name was going on down here?

The truth is, there were no mercenaries. Only the compound guards were in the jungle. Our own guards were assigned to encircle the compound and fire their weapons. They, too, believed that we were threatened. Every White Night, Jim sent a different team into the rain forest to fire shots. Each boy was unaware that there had been others before him creating the same panic. Each was told a different story, one he could not repeat. No one realized that all of the gunfire was from our guns.

It is, of course, only in hindsight, in the safety of sanity, that I am able to see Jim's deceit. He alone knew that there was no real threat. We were blinded by fear and isolation. Physically weak from malnutrition and lack of sleep and mentally exhausted from constant fear of punishment, we were feeble, compliant automatons. In madness there is no way to think logically.

I Was Rewarded for My Loyalty

As the days wore on, I struggled to preserve what was left of my sanity. I became accustomed to the White Nights and suicide drills. At first they occurred once a month, then there seemed to be one every two weeks and they would last for several days. My only solace was working in the fields. I felt grounded when we were planting or foraging. It was there in the sun and its ravaging heat that we had a purpose. In the field, there was something tangible to hold on to.

Yet again, my discipline and application were noticed and rewarded. At Carolyn's suggestion Father moved me out of my crowded cabin and into the one his three sons shared with

Beth, his daughter-in-law. There were a few mixed-gender cabins. Most were inhabited by the bold young teenagers who wanted to live with a girlfriend or boyfriend. They spent all their spare time, Sunday evenings, to build them. With only four hours of light available to hammer and saw, it would take months.

As I passed my favorite latrine, which was new and relatively fly-free, I wondered why it was taking so long to build more cabins. We were so overcrowded. I recalled that the lavatory had been built in only a day and its construction was no more difficult than our stilted cabins. What were our goals? Was there a master plan for the hundreds of hardworking inhabitants of this land?

The fact that Jim had approved my move was a sign that trust was slowly being bestowed upon me. It was an honor to live with Jim's sons. Father couldn't let just anyone cohabitate with them. They often talked back to him and an untrustworthy individual might try to profit by using their adolescent rebelliousness against them. Father could not afford to have his sons confronted for speaking up against him in private. He was very concerned about their self-confidence. This was one of the reasons he had sent Stephan and Lew ahead to Jonestown. Another sign of his trust in me was the fact that I now had access to guns because his sons were on the security team.

Lew, Jim's handsome twenty-two-year-old adopted Korean son, and his wife Beth were easy to live with. His other adopted sons, Tim, eighteen, and Jimmy Junior, seventeen, one white and the other black, were hardly ever at the cabin. Stephan, his biological son, was nineteen years old and lived in another cabin, but came by frequently to visit his brothers. Only Beth and I were there at night, but at dawn, the boys would stomp in, tired and worn after guarding the compound all night.

While they talked, yawned, and undressed, Beth would head over to the nursery to hold her twenty-month-old son,

Chioke, before going on to her job in the laundry. I thought it was sad that Jim forbade parents to keep their children with them at night but I knew it was for their own safety in the event of an attack that they remained in the guarded children's dorm. Children and seniors lived close to the Pavilion—a curse because it meant having to live next to the center of insanity. The loudspeaker system, although still audible, was less intrusive where we lived.

Eating and Staying Clean

When I rose, it didn't take much effort to get dressed since I slept almost completely clothed. We had to be prepared in case of an emergency invasion by our enemies. The early mornings were cool. The cries of the howler monkeys that had frightened me on my arrival had become a soothing constant in the midst of our uncertain situation. Jim said bras were a Western indoctrination, so I pulled a shirt over my bare chest, even though it hurt to go braless.

I was thankful to the Greeting Committee, which I privately referred to as the "Confiscation Committee," for sparing my thick wool socks. Not only did they keep my feet dry, they warded off mosquito bites from my ankles and the bottoms of my feet. My boots were deteriorating, but hopefully they would hold out until I was to leave. The small hole on one side was working itself into a tear, large enough for the dreaded red biting ant to get access to my toes.

On most mornings, when I stepped down from my bunk onto the wooden planks, something soft and warm touched my foot. It was Beth's bear, which had fallen from its hiding place in her bed. Each of us had a secret something we cherished. It could be as egotistical and vain as a mirror or as functional as my socks, but it was something we'd managed to keep for ourselves. For Beth, the bear was probably the closest thing she had to being with her baby. Placing the curly-haired teddy next to her head, I would grab my sickle and tiptoe out of our cabin into the dawn's fresh, revitalizing air.

I was still working in the fields. By now I had learned to overcome physical discomfort at any cost, and I thought of the grain bugs in the rice as friends—my own little protein-boosters.

On some days our field work involved foraging for edible shrubs along the jungle's extremity. I always concentrated on finding a special green leaf, the one Mary, the magical chef, and her kitchen staff used for our Sunday-only vegetables, my favorite treat. There was also an extraordinary purple root, which we used to season other rare dishes. Mary's special leaves, the long, mossy, green one with blood-red spines, were always hidden under a faint emerald mother shrub with bright saffron flecks. I moved forward, squatting, my knees growing sore, diligently searching.

We always carried empty burlap sacks with us to the work-site. They smelled of previous gatherings from different fields. Sometimes a hint of pineapple wafted up into my nostrils, other times sugarcane. We filled sack after sack with sustenance for our comrades, heaved them onto our heads, and transported them back out to the clearing.

As the mornings passed slowly into noon, I would begin to feel weak, hungry for the cassava bread and plantain sandwich sitting on a burnt log where I'd thrown my outer shirt. The ants never attacked our food; probably the strange-smelling additive kept them away. I liked the plantain, from the banana family. It was slightly sweet, its texture thick and filling, reminding me of the sweet potato pies I'd eaten after our revival meetings and at Mary's home, so very long ago.

When I didn't dream of food, I fantasized about my shower, how I'd rinse the dirt off my body, the water dripping onto my shoulders, gently running over my breasts, in dark muddy rivers that poured down my legs and onto my feet.

Planning one's shower was important because showers also had restrictions. Anyone reported to have allowed the water to run longer than two minutes was assigned to the Learning Crew for a day. But one especially pleasant grandmother, Clara, usually gave me an extra minute by acting as if another person was already taking a shower when I got there.

"One more minute!" she'd yell, as I jumped in and took that one minute of no one's time, just to get an extra rinse.

I didn't know how the cold water was transported from the river, but it was preciously rationed. Never wanting to waste a speck of the precious liquid, I stripped, then lined up my toiletries neatly on the wooden planks next to my feet so that they were immediately accessible. Quickly and carefully I turned on the water and rinsed briskly. Not much water was needed, I got my body just wet enough to lather my head and torso. Another quick rinse and I continued to lather the crusted dirt from my arms and legs. Once well soaped, I turned the faucet on again and relished the ecstasy of the cold water running all over me. I was always cautious to keep my mouth shut in the shower while the water ran over my face so that I wouldn't swallow any and get sick.

Even with all the rules, taking a shower was luxurious. After drying off, I would change into my only other outfit, an oversized T-shirt, and step out. Looking over my shoulder to make sure I was alone, I would lean over and hug my secret accomplice, who was still seated at the entrance of the showers.

What Would Life Be Like Without Father?

Every now and then, my daydreams were interrupted by a welcome rumbling sound. Emanating from the northern part of the forest and working its thunderous way toward us would be a rain squall. Its winds would cool the air and the intensity of the downpour was usually so great we had no choice but to take a break, a glorious respite that could last ten minutes.

During the rainy season, if we were lucky, several rains would come in a day. They would drench the trees' upper canopy, turning the leaves into channels that funneled the liquid of life downward to the forest floor in a wondrous roar. Massive leaves would sway up and down until the cloudburst moved on, farther south, and then the quiet resumed. Once more the sun would shine down upon us, steam from the rains would filter back up into the atmosphere, and we would continue to labor on until sunset.

One day, the Learning Crew worked through a downpour. Not only were these downtrodden cast-offs praised for their stamina, each of them was miraculously released from the crew for having proved that they were correct thinkers. Once branded sinners, the former crew members were now revered as the devout, and they seemed to hold grudges toward anyone who had not lived through the hell they had experienced.

The rules changed after this incident, and no one was allowed to break during the day anymore. If the rains came, we worked through them, even if we couldn't see the ground. But in our eleven-hour days of hoeing, raking, planting, foraging, burning, or clearing land, there were fleeting moments of relief. On some evenings instead of hiking back in, the flatbed truck came out and carried us, worn and weary, back to the center of the compound. Above us a crimson, orange, and turquoise Guyanese sky would melt around our sorry crew as we jerked and bounced back and forth on the rutted dirt road, and I would fantasize about how wonderful it would be to see such a sunset someday away from Jonestown, someplace safe and free. . . .

I looked around at my work crew, all of us up since dawn with the screeching of the howler monkeys, working the fields until dusk, each of us expecting so much more from our lives and futures than this. But it was getting too late for dreams. Our spirits were weakening and our hopes were being deliberately drained from us. Jim's arsenal of manipulation and deceit was stripping away our dignity, ensuring our numbed allegiance and unquestioning loyalty.

When there was a minute of solitude I often wondered what life would be like without Father. I loved the natural tranquility of the interior, the dark, frothy river so close, just through the trees, yet inaccessible. Our cabins, tin-roofed and small, could have housed families, lovers, children with their parents, but instead we were partitioned into nonbonding arrangements. Like the inmates of a prison camp, we could not make close contacts. There was no one to confide in, no one to whisper to in the middle of the night, no one to make plans with, no one to trust. And solitude was disallowed because it too was dangerous. Time alone could lead to introspection and capitalistic thoughts.

Visiting My Mother Was Dangerous

I was always afraid of how Jim would perceive my visits to Mama: too often, too long, too early, not late enough. There was a fine line between too little and too much empathy. Too much compassion meant you'd break under torture and questioning by the enemy. Too little proved you could become a turncoat and traitor to Father. I'd learned to walk the fine line. But my feelings about Mama were chaotic. I loved her and hated myself because my love for her weakened my dedication to the Cause. I was disgusted by the panic I felt when I thought she'd get us both into trouble. I was always fighting with myself over each decision to see or not to see her. Sometimes I selfishly believed she was a drain on me, a weight that pulled me deeper into confusion and self-loathing each time I visited. If I stayed away from her, I would be viewed as loyal and unencumbered by the dangerous "worldly" pettiness of family ties. But I had to struggle with severe guilt as a daughter.

When I resolved to sneak a visit to Mama's, I usually lay on her cot talking softly as she sat at my side. And the next thing I knew, I would find myself being gently awakened by Mama's protective voice.

"Debbie. . . Debbie, honey. It's been a couple of hours, you better get up now." I would slowly focus upon Mama's worried face, her eyes filled with sorrow.

"Oh, Mama, you shouldn't have let me sleep. Now we won't have time to visit." As I got up to leave she'd beg me to eat the hardboiled eggs she'd saved up from her senior's allotment, not satisfied until we shared an egg together.

"No, Mama, you need this to keep up your health," I would protest. But she would not give in.

"Debbie, they have you working too hard. I want to tell Father this is not good for you. They do not feed you kids enough protein for this type of work."

"Mama, please. Promise me you won't protest."

"The meetings are too long and I'm concerned about the way he has those children spanked and punished. It's not right to subject the children to the Well or the Box."

"Mama, whatever you believe or want to say, it must only be said to me," I kept urging her. "Promise me, Mama, tell *no one* but me your fears and concerns. These will be our secrets. Otherwise you will be confronted, Mama. Tell no one!!!!"

I longed to confide in her. But to tell Mama I wanted to leave would mean burdening her with knowledge of a treasonous thought and she could be brutally punished for not telling. No, it was too dangerous. Even the most innocent and caring of people had harmed a loved one by naïvely misspeaking their minds to Father. I couldn't tell anyone because they would have thought I had been assigned to test their loyalties. I was the perfect disciple; after all I had been one of Father's trusted few in the United States, and now I lived in the cabin with his sons. There was no one I could tell. I resolved never to share my thoughts, never to trust anyone, and to play the game by their rules.

I was increasingly worried for Mama. I had begun to see her fears and stress as new lines and dark marks under her eyes. She was not sleeping well. Fear was making her agitated, quick to jump at little sounds. As the world around us became more malevolent I felt she was in danger and could become a danger to me. She and Mary had already made a grievous mistake of judgment in an incident the previous week.

Mary had concocted a wonderful jam, made of some tropical fruit she must have secretly gathered. It tasted like marmalade and was just as orange. Mama had served it to me on a few occasions, furtively pulling out Mary's gift and spreading the preserves on the cassava bread she had saved from breakfast.

The Last Straw

The ugly incident happened on a night after several days free of suicide drills. All of our spirits were lighter than usual. Father was laughing in his infectious, high-pitched cackle and life felt as though it might be beginning to look up at last. I was sitting with Stephan, laughing at his impersonation of his dad's chuckle, when Mary decided to bring her elixir to the podium for Father to taste. On nights like these Father would be joking with the children or relieving the miserable sods who'd been sentenced to the Learning Crew, telling them they had proved themselves and were no longer restricted. Everyone felt less apprehensive when Father seemed to be okay again.

Mary, sensing the light mood, stepped onto Father's platform to address him at the public microphone.

"Yes, Mary. . . . What is it you'd like to say on this gloriously calm evening?"

"Father, I've somethin' here I want you to taste." She made her way up to his chair.

"What's this?" He raised his eyebrows, pulled down his reading glasses, and smiled.

"It's a treat I've been workin' on, Father. . . . Yes, sir . . . and Lisa's been my taster and says it's good enough to sell in the capital."

With gracious pride she handed the tiny orange jar to Father. Out from her apron pocket appeared a spoon and Father took a wee lick.

I watched, delighted.

Like a snake, Father flicked his tongue into the concoction.

"What an extravagance!" he spat. "How much time have you wasted on this?" My blood curdled. "Where did you get the fruit to make this?" he screamed. Mary shuffled back slightly, away from Father's spraying spittle. Terrified, I pinched Stephan's finger. Without a warning, "little Lisa," my mama, stood up in courageous defense of Mary.

"Oh, Father, Mary's marmalade is sweet, good, and it's marketable. . . . I think you could learn to truly enjoy it."

"Shut up, woman," he yelled. "I want Mary to answer from which field she stole the fruit to make this bourgeois extravagance!"

But his anger had been diverted and he turned from Mary, still seething.

"How *daarrreee* you!" He glared at Mama. "Are you arguing with *meee*? Are you telling Father, I am mistaken?"

"Father knows what's good," yelled an anxious voice. Someone grabbed Mama's thin shoulders, trying to get her out of Father's view, praying he'd lose his train of thought if he couldn't see her. Father admonished the crowd.

"Quiet! Silence!"

Everyone froze as he rose from his chair and glared down at Mama's small frame.

"Lisa . . . you dare to challenge me?" he sneered. "Let this be a warning to you. You are no different from the rest of us!" Mama remained standing as was required during confrontation. I sat in silence, a paralyzed coward, too afraid to stand and defend innocence.

I tried to think. Father's anger did not fit the crime. He was speaking to me! Through his actions toward Mama he was warning me. Perhaps he had seen me giggling with Stephan earlier that night. I could hear his previous admonitions reverberate in my head. . . . "I will punish those closest to you if you ever deceive or hurt me." Father was letting me know that he had tired of his charade of concern for my mother. She was just another soldier who needed correcting and punishment.

"Get out!" screamed the inner voice I had systematically silenced for so long. "Find a way to get both of us out."

Chapter 2

Leaving Cults

Growing Up in a Cult

Flore Astid

In this brief narrative, Flore Astrid, a former cult member, describes being brought up in a cult and not having the skills to survive in the outside world when she decided to leave. She describes how being in a cult did not prepare her for life 'outside' and that once she left, she found herself making a number of painful mistakes trying to figure out who she was and where she belonged. Eventually she discovered people like herself who did not fit into traditional societal expectations, and she has learned that even the most painful experiences can be opportunities to become wiser if one is open to them.

For me, the experience of growing up in a cult has been like a two-edged sword, inflicting some nasty wounds but providing me with a powerful tool to cut through the lies and illusions that seem to make up the greater part of our reality structure.

As a child, I learned at a relatively early age that "reality" is anything but concrete and objective, but is rather moulded through our own developmental process, largely reflecting who we are more than anything solid "out there." In my case, I had two realities to contend with, the cult world and the outside world, and like many other cult kids, I was taught that the former was good or "heavenly" and the latter was bad, or "satanic."

For different reasons, I never really felt at home in the cult, I tried to believe but something in me just couldn't accept their "truth." Having moved constantly due to cult activities made it difficult for me to slide into the outside world so I ended up being the freak in the group no matter which side

I took. I was extremely lonely (being an only child didn't help much either) and as I entered puberty I became both depressive and at times even suicidal.

No Tools to Deal with Life

Leaving the cult wasn't exactly easy, even though my father had also left and provided a lot of support. I had been somewhat overprotected most of my life so that the tools I needed to navigate the outside world simply hadn't been developed. I have always had my brains to count on, but that didn't stop me from making really stupid mistakes later on. I had no respect for myself, couldn't set limits and was open to trying pretty much anything that had been forbidden in the cult. I guess I just had to learn the hard way (and still am!). By the time I left the cult for good I had become extremely destructive, and went through a long series of painful lessons trying to find a place for myself on this strange planet which to me still seems more like a collective loony bin than a place called home.

Today I have found a small corner in the world where I feel, if not at home, at least somewhat comfortable with my surroundings and myself. My friends have become my family, and luckily I have quite a few (mostly misfits and outsiders like myself). I also have a son who keeps me from being too destructive and [that] is in itself a good reason to stay alive. I guess he saves me from myself. I live alone, not being very good at relationships; they usually don't last longer than a year (I never really learned how to "bond" with anyone and intimacy scares me).

Out of Painful Experiences Comes Growth

Recently, I gave a talk about my experiences to a large and sympathetic group. It was very empowering since for the first time I was able to express my feelings in a caring environment and discovered that I was not alone, many cult survivors have had similar experiences to mine. I think the whole healing process can be speeded up substantially when there is an opportunity to work through one's difficulties in therapy or at least with others who have been through a similar ordeal. I never had that chance, so I basically had to heal myself (can't afford therapy and where I live there is little expertise on cult issues in general).

Part of my healing process has been to see how even the most painful experiences can be used to grow and become wiser if one is open to learning the lessons hidden within each hardship. I don't see myself as a victim, I have learned to see through lies and develop spiritually on my own terms. I guess I made the best out of what I got.

Some say that the greatest lessons are also the most painful, and growing up as a cult kid has certainly taught me a lot. Finding the strength to carry on hasn't always been easy, but I've made it this far and I certainly don't plan on giving up now. I just hope others like me may be as fortunate.

I Left Children of God to Keep My Children Safe

Miriam Williams

Started by David Berg, also known as Moses David, the Children of God cult was formed in the late 1960s. It attracted many alternative lifestyle seekers who had become disillusioned with the hippie movement by appealing to a new form of Christianity. In her memoir about being in the Children of God, Miriam Williams examines her own experiences in the cult, from being proselytized to eventually leaving due to the bizarre and perverse sexual practices and activities that emerged over the course of her eighteen years as a member. One of its most alarming practices was called "flirty fishing" in which sex was shown to be an expression of God's love. By promoting this as a Christian practice, Moses David convinced women in the cult to become prostitutes as a method of attracting new converts and raising money for the cult's survival. Besides being part of a prostitution ring, Williams was forced into an arranged marriage. Her eventual disillusionment with the cult arose when she discovered that children were being exposed to pornographic images through videos, letters, drawings, and photographs. It is this discovery, which Williams recounts in this excerpt from her book, that made her evaluate whether or not she could continue being a member.

It was September 1986. I was thirty-three years old, giving birth to my fifth child in a hospital in Pordenone [Italy]. The nurses were excited, since I had agreed to use a new birthing chair they had bought and none of the local Italian women would try it out. I told them I would much rather sit

Miriam Williams, *Heaven's Harlots: My Fifteen Years as a Sacred Prostitute in the Children of God Cult*, New York: Eagle Brook, William Morrow and Company, 1998.

during birth than lie down. When the contractions came hard and strong, they put me in the chair, only no one had taken the time to figure out the complicated stirrup and strap system. The cold metal felt icy next to my hot, sweaty skin, and while they tried adjusting the stirrups up and down and over again, I held my legs open, pressed tightly to the sides of my bloated stomach, and pushed and pushed. Out came my second son.

[My husband] Paolo wanted to give him an Italian name, so we called him Michelangelo, after the great Florentine painter.

After Emma's departure, we enjoyed a few months of raising our children with a few lowly but sweet Family [how the cult referred to itself] members. Our peace was short-lived, with the unfortunate arrival of two new leaders. Judah was an American who claimed to have a degree in journalism. He was a cynical man and his large, bearded face showed little sign of empathy or compassion. His wife, Anna, a thick-skinned Italian beauty, had not borne children gracefully. Thankfully, we never shared with any of these Family members since we were supposedly not engaging in any sexual sharing between couples due to the venereal diseases that were spreading around the Family. Adults entering Europe from Eastern countries were particularly told not to share at all. On the other hand, the letters about having sex with underage teens were explicit. A series of letters supposedly written by Mo [movement founder Berg] about a fictional future end-time supergirl named Heaven's Girl was circulating among our teens. In these illustrated letters the young teen has multiple sexual relationships with men of all ages. With each new letter that arrived, I became more worried. Heaven's Girl became a sex fanatic. Then a new series titled Heaven's Girl was sent out with an artist's depiction of Mo in bed with a teenager. I confronted our new leaders immediately on their opinions of these letters. They were conveniently vague.

I'm Here Because the Father of My Child Is Here

"What do you think?" asked Judah, without batting an eyelid.

It was a moment of truth and I failed miserably. If I confessed that I didn't approve of Mo or any adult man sleeping with teenagers, I might as well leave the Family, which was an option I had not yet discussed with my husband. Paolo and I never talked about the implications of these letters. Parents in the Family had become like the people we had despised when we were young revolutionaries—those who "turn their head, pretending they just don't hear," as Bob Dylan says in "Blowing in the Wind." I wanted to make sure my own children were safe now, and later I would address the issue of what was going on in other homes. At the same time, by accepting a deviant collective conscience, I was beginning to doubt my own virtue.

"I think it's Dad and Mamma's business what they do in their household. He is supposed to be the Prophet. But I don't want my girls exposed to adult sex. Is that clear?" I answered.

"Don't you think that Mo is God's Prophet for the Endtime?" asked Anna, completely avoiding the question.

"Actually, I have serious doubts about that, yes. But whether Mo is a Prophet or not doesn't bother me at all. What bothers me is people taking Mo's letters as if they were God's Word. And if you really want to know, I don't even believe everything in the Bible is God's Word either. A lot has been tampered with through the ages."

"Why are you in the Family then?" asked Judah suspiciously.

"I'm in the Family for the community. I'm in here because I still think it's better than the system. And right this minute, I'm in here because this is where the father of my children is. I lost one child, and I don't want to lose any more."

"No wonder you guys are doing so badly. And we were told it was Paolo," replied Judah, rubbing his chin as if that discovery took a lot of mental effort.

"Well, it's me. But I'm also the one who got us this house you are living in. And if you want to stay here, I want to know what you think about sex with children."

"You have no right to come in here and demand us to answer your questions," shouted Judah. "You made your point. Don't worry. I won't touch your precious little girls."

I Began to Wonder Why I Was Here

The Family was not free of the bureaucratic problems found in the system. I wasn't in this hierarchy, but I still had minimal power in my own house. I spoke to Paolo about my conversation with Judah, but he thought I was imagining things. Since our children slept with us, in our own bedroom, he said we had nothing to worry about. The letters about sex and children did not seem to bother him so much. He said that it wasn't really having sex. Mo never said to have actual intercourse with children! Like most of us, he probably did not read these perverse letters, but they were there, like a cancer eating any ideals we had left.

Everyone I talked to convinced me that I was taking these letters too seriously. I began to think that I really had a problem after all. But what problem was it? I thought about it for hours as I lay awake in bed at night. I recalled an incident that had happened about a year before, when my mother and sister Karen were visiting me in Italy while we were alone at Paolo's hometown. Karen mentioned that it was terrible how we let the children run around naked on the beach. Actually, most of the Europeans do that also. We got into a heated discussion about nudity, and finally she said what was on her mind.

"I read that the adults in your group show their naked body parts to their children, as a way of sex education. Is that true?"

Suddenly, as if a window of my past life had been opened, I saw my father showing me his penis.

"Well, what's so bad about that? Dad used to do it," I answered.

"Oh, you're disgusting! Dad never did that! You're just making that up because you're in this group! You're sick!"

She talked to my mother about this, since my mom and dad had already been separated when she was still a little girl. My mother assured her that it was not true. Coincidentally, my mother also had a severe epileptic attack while she was visiting at this time. I don't remember if it was before or after this conversation. It bothered me so much that I closed that window to the deep past.

As I lay in bed and recalled this event, I thought perhaps I was afraid of something in my past. Not one of the other adults living with us seemed as concerned about sex and children as I was. I did seem to have a problem with sex. Maybe it was I who was perverted by an evil and sick mind. On the other hand, those who did not like the Mo letters left the Family. What was I doing here anyway?

I had a lot of time to think about it. Soon after my outburst with our new leaders, I was restricted to my room for two hours of extra word time and prayer a day. I welcomed this restriction since I used it to get much needed sleep. But I also did a lot more thinking than praying, and I didn't read the Bible or Mo letters. Why did I still let leaders tell me what to do? Because I had grown accustomed to it maybe? It was a habit—part of living communally. But why did I live this way? My ideals were gone. My curiosity about a different lifestyle had long been satiated. Like Alice in Wonderland, I had seen enough. My dream was over. I came to the conclusion that I was only in the Family now because Paolo wanted to stay. I had to convince Paolo to leave.

I Discovered More Reasons to Leave

However, Paolo seemed to find life in the Family easier than life in the Italian system. Although he worked hard, he had no rigid work hours, and all responsibilities were shared by a group of adults. If money ran low, we had a choice of going out as witnessing teams to sell tapes or singing in restaurants. Paolo was also convinced that the system was a bad place to raise children. Because of his own traumatic experiences as a child, which had left him and his brother with forms of depression, he did not want his children to have the same condition. Two of his cousins had died drug-induced deaths. He saw the Family as a haven from a cruel world. He appeared to like having rules and regulations to guide his every act so that he didn't have to think, make decisions, or take the blame for anything. Even though I know he did not agree with the letters either, he truly believed that his children were safe here.

Unlike Alice, I could not seize the tablecloth in my hands and shake everybody off. This was real life—not a dream! I spent a few months vacillating in my ruminations about who was crazy, I or they. In my weakened state, I was reproached by Judah and his wife for making Paolo use condoms, which I had recently insisted upon, so he stopped using them and I became pregnant immediately.

When I was about three months pregnant, Judah and his family moved to another home. We were expecting a new family soon, and I started cleaning out the bedrooms upstairs in preparation. As I went through the drawers in the children's rooms, where Judah's girls had slept, I came across a spiral notebook. I thought I could reuse it for school if there were enough empty pages, so I leafed through it. The name of his oldest girl, who was about eight, was written on the first page.

I turned another page, and the drawing leaped up at me as if I had been grabbed around the throat and choked.

There, drawn in pencil, was the replication of a fully erect penis.

I gasped. I shut the book and breathed deeply, trying not to scream. What had gotten into me? I had seen drawings of penises in Mo letters before. But this was a child's book. And it appeared to be drawn from looking at a live model. The detail was too precise. I opened the book and frantically searched through the other pages. It was full of penis drawings, at different stages of erection.

"Oh my God!" I thought to myself. "Did this happen in my house? Was a little innocent girl taught to draw her daddy's penis while I was sleeping in the next room? What a horrible person I am. And how much have my own daughters been exposed to?" Athena was seven years old. Was she included in these lessons?

I Knew I Had to Protect My Children

I took the book as evidence and went to the window to check on the kids. Athena was playing on the swing we had hung under a spreading oak tree. Genvieve was dressed up in her long princess dress, playing at some fantasy about being married to a prince. She had long, curly blond hair, and whenever a small boy visited our home, my four-year-old would make him be a prince. She lived in a fantasy world. Jordan was by the fountain, throwing flowers, leaves, and bugs she found into the pool that had formed from the running fountain water. I couldn't believe that my precious little ones had been touched by this evil. From a deep recess in my soul, the part that I had shut off because of a long-ago pain, I had a premonition of repeated history. I did not know what it meant, but I knew I had to protect my children. Michelangelo was asleep in his cot. At barely a year old, he had been touched by none of this. And I was never going to let that chance come. I gathered up the children's passports and hid them in the pages of one of my books. I took the book outside and hid it again in the barn. That evening I confronted Paolo, showing him the horrible notebook drawings.

"We don't know that these were drawn by her, or that they were even drawn here," he said, pushing the notebook aside as if to take it out of his sight and so out of his mind.

"Of course, they were drawn by her," I protested. "And so what if they were not drawn here in this house. This is pornography. What if Athena saw this?"

"You don't think Athena has seen the Mo letters?"

I realized with a gasp how foolish and blinded I had been. What was to stop the children from looking at the Mo books with fully detailed sex organs drawn for the adult readers, or so I wanted to believe. And even the children's newest comic books from the Family, the much-read Heaven's Girl series, included the naked man's body. He was right. Athena had seen pictures like this.

"But this has been drawn by a little girl! Don't you see the difference?"

"What are you worried about? They're gone now!"

"But they'll send more leaders to us. Paolo, I don't want my children exposed to this. I'm leaving."

"Where are you going? And how are you getting there?" Paolo laughed, knowing I could not drive.

"I'm writing my mother. She will send me money to leave Italy. I have the children's passports, Paolo. I'm leaving."

Paolo's face dropped. He looked in the drawer and saw that our passports were gone.

"I'll find them," he said weakly.

"No, you won't. And what can you do? I have proof, just like Jerry did. I can get the kids if we go to court. But I know what it's like to have a child taken from me, and I won't put you through that pain, Paolo. I'm leaving, but you can come if you want to."

Paolo softened drastically before my eyes. I knew I would make it out.

It Was Decided That We Would Leave

"What will I do for work?" asked Paolo. "We've been in the Family for years now. I can't borrow money again from my family. How will we live?"

I felt truly sorry for Paolo, especially since I had introduced him to the Family to begin with. But I knew it was Paolo who had decided to go back, so now I would make this decision without my ever-imposing guilt feelings.

"Are you saying you will leave the Family for good?" I asked.

"I'll follow you and the kids, not because I want to but because you are making me."

It took a few more weeks to encourage Paolo to do this. A new family had come to the farmhouse, and it seemed like everything would be fine again. Paolo tried to convince me that Judah was a special case, but now that my eyes were opened to the reality of the Mo letters, I saw sexual innuendos everywhere. I was insistent. Many years later, when we had been out of the Family for years, I asked Paolo why he had wanted to stay in a group where there might have been child abuse.

"I did like everyone else," he answered without hesitation. "I put it out of my mind. I thought this would never happen to us. We all thought, well, it didn't happen to us. And living in a community gave me security. I didn't know how I would get a job if I left or how to support my family. The community gives you security."

Finally, we left in our RV. Paolo was still complaining about how he was going to support us all. He told the new people that we were only going on a faith trip and we would be back. Everyone knew I was having problems. I was also pregnant, and pregnant women, everyone knew, sometimes act funny.

I didn't care what they thought of me. I had enough thoughts of my own. Should I stay with Paolo? He was the father of the kids, after all. And he was so weak. Maybe I would stay with him until the kids were a little older. At least I would stay until the baby was born. I couldn't make any decisions now. All I wanted to do was get away.

There were about eighteen thousand members in the Family at that time. There were now six fewer.

I Left Aum Shinrikyo After the Gas Attacks

Hidetoshi Takahashi

As a long-time member of Aum Shinrikyo, the Japanese cult responsible for the gas attacks on the Tokyo subway, Hidetoshi Takahashi explains in an interview what his reasons for joining the cult were and why he began expressing doubts about its practices. One of Aum's most compelling tenets, he claims, was its apocalyptic vision that attracted many people who wanted to renounce the material world. After participating in a ritual known as "Christ Initiation," however, in which renunciates were made to take drugs to reach a higher level of existence, Takahashi started to question the cult's appeal. He began expressing doubts to his superiors and was told to believe the leader and do what he says. Being given a job to collect seismologic information led him to witness the inner workings of the cult's leadership, which caused him even more concern. Takahashi claims it was because he was in the lower echelons of the group that he was not asked to participate in the attacks on the subway, which killed twelve people and injured countless others. After the attacks occurred, he immediately left the cult but he still maintains interest in Aum and attended the trial of its leader, Shoko Asahara. This entry was excerpted from a chapter that includes a longer version.

At college I felt a deep alienation between my outer and my inner self. I was a cheerful, enthusiastic person with lots of friends, but once I was alone in my room, I was engulfed by loneliness and there was nobody I could share that world with.

Hidetoshi Takahashi, *Underground: The Tokyo Gas Attack and the Japanese Psyche*, London: The Harvill Press, 2000. Translated from the Japanese by Alfred Birnbaum and Philip Gabriel.

I've been that way since childhood. I remember always going inside the closet when I was a child. I didn't want to see my parents, and even in my own room I didn't feel like I had my own space. When you're a child it feels like your parents are always interfering. For me the only place to escape to and find peace was the closet. Granted it's a strange habit, but alone there in the darkness I could feel my consciousness grow razor sharp. It's just you alone, face-to-face with yourself in the dark. In a sense, then, I was drawn to something like the Aum retreats since I was little.

In junior high I liked to listen to progressive rock. Pink Floyd's *The Wall*, for example. Definitely not the sort of music I'd recommend unless you want something to bring you down. I found out about [Armenian-Greek mystic G.I.] Gurdjieff through [the rock group] King Crimson. Their guitarist Robert Fripp was a follower of Gurdjieff. After he got into that his music changed drastically. I think much of my outlook on life was influenced by that kind of music.

At high school I was into sports, basketball and badminton, but after entering college I felt I had to draw a line between myself and society. I was what we call a "Moratorium Person": someone who doesn't want to grow up. Our generation grew up after Japan had become a wealthy country and we viewed society through this lens of affluence. I just couldn't adjust to the "adult society" I saw outside. It seemed warped to me somehow. Wasn't there some other way to live your life, some other way of viewing the world? During my college days I had a lot of free time, and was preoccupied with these questions.

When you're young you have all kinds of idealistic notions in your head, but coming face-to-face with the realities of your own life makes you see how immature you are. I felt very frustrated.

To free myself, to make a fresh start, I poked my nose into all sorts of things, hoping to find the energy I needed to live.

Life is full of suffering, and the contradictions in the real world irked me. To escape these, I imagined my own sort of utopian society, which made it easier for me to be taken in by a religious group that espoused a similar vision.

Aum Promoted an Apocalyptic Vision

When the Aum question comes up, people always start talking about relations between parents and children going sour, and family discord, but it can't be reduced to something so simplistic. Certainly one of the attractions of Aum lay in people's frustrations with reality and unrest in the family, but a much more important factor lies in apocalyptic feelings of "the end of the world," feelings all of us have about the future. If you pay attention to the universal feeling of all of us, all Japanese—all humankind, even—then you can't explain Aum's appeal to so many people by saying it's all based on discord in the family. . . .

It might be hard to generalize . . . , but I think inside all Japanese there is an apocalyptic viewpoint: an invisible, unconscious sense of fear. When I say that all Japanese have this fear I mean some people have already pulled aside the veil, while others have yet to do so. If this veil were suddenly drawn back everyone would feel a sense of terror about the near future, the direction our world's heading in. Society is the foundation stone for people's lives, and they don't know what's going to happen to it in the future. This feeling grows stronger the more affluent a country becomes. It's like a dark shadow looming larger and larger. . . .

When I was at school Nostradamus's *Prophecies* became famous, and that sense that "The End Is Nigh" wedged itself deep into my consciousness through the mass media. And I wasn't the only one to feel like that. I don't want this to deteriorate into some simplistic theory about "my generation," but I feel very strongly that all Japanese at that time had the idea drilled into them of 1999 being the end of the world. Aum renunciates have already accepted, inside themselves, the end of the world, because when they become a renunciate, they discard themselves totally, thereby abandoning the world. In other words, Aum is a collection of people who have accepted the end. People who continue to hold out hope for the near future still have an attachment to the world. If you have attachments, you won't discard your Self, but for renunciates it's as if they've leaped right off a cliff. And taking a giant leap like that feels good. They lose something—but gain something in return.

Therefore the idea of "the End" is one of the axes around which Aum Shinrikyo revolved. "Armageddon's coming, so become a renunciate," they urged, "donate all your money to Aum"—and of course that became their source of income. . . .

[Psychiatrist] Robert Jay Lifton has said that there are many cults that have an apocalyptic creed, but Aum is the only one that marched straight toward it as part of their program. That makes sense to me.

Even now there's an element about Aum, its driving force and direction, that I can't fully understand. It had such tremendous energy, and pulled in so many people—including me, of course. But how did it do this?

Aum Leader Claimed He Had Been Poisoned

When I was at college many new religions tried to convert me, but in terms of grappling with the direction the world had taken, seriously formulating a religious worldview, searching earnestly for a lifestyle that fit this view, and then rigorously putting it into practice, Aum stood out head and shoulders above the rest. Aum was the most amazing group of all. I really admired them for the way they practiced what they preached. Compared to them, other religions were resigned, cozy, comfortable, passive. Aum training was very, very tough. Their religious view—that you must transform your own body before you can transform the world—had a hard-hitting realism. If there's any chance for salvation, I thought, it has to begin like this.

To give you an example, with the shortage of food in the world, if only everyone, bit by bit, reduced their consumption the way the Aum diet does, then this food problem would be solved. Not by increasing the supply, but by changing the body, because Aum people eat only a tiny amount of food. If mankind is going to live in harmony with the earth, we've reached the age when we have to start thinking in this way. . . .

When I joined I was put to work straightaway making Cosmo cleaners. Aum was already claiming that it was being attacked from the outside with sarin gas, and Cosmo cleaners were designed to reduce the toxicity. Just prior to my taking vows the Leader gave a sermon. "I've been hit with poison gas," he told us, coughing and coughing. He was as limp as a rag doll, and his face was all dark. It seemed tremendously real. "I can only last another month," he said, "and at this rate Aum will be destroyed. Before this happens, I want those who believe in me to gather around me. All of you will serve as my shield." It was a powerful sermon. It forced lay followers to question their faith: here is the Leader in such dire straits and you're just sitting around? How can you call this faith? All at once about three hundred people took vows, and I was one of them, caught up in this wave. Things started to look strange to me when I was forced to undergo what they called "Christ Initiation." All the followers were made to take drugs. Any way you look at it, the whole thing was carelessly done. Using drugs in the name of religion, in order to enter some elevated state, is suspect in itself, but even supposing you accept it as a legitimate means, at the very least you've got to do it in an organized fashion. What they gave us was something close to LSD, I suspect, and for almost everyone it was their first such experience. Some people went crazy and were just left to their own devices. That really troubled me. Even if the Leader had planned this as a method of elevating our spiritual state, the way it was handled left a lot to be desired.

I felt a great deal of resistance to this whole "Christ Initiation," and after I went through it I struggled with whether or not I should leave Aum. It was such a shock it drove me to tears. "What the hell do they think they're doing?" I wondered. It wasn't just me—even a few of the leadership wavered over this initiation, some of the enlightened practitioners who hung on Asahara's every word. It felt like Aum was starting to fall apart.

I Started Having Doubts

I think I joined Aum as a kind of adventure. You have to be a bit forgiving of a system organized to open up an entirely unknown world for you . . . so I did accept that system. On the one hand I wanted to adjust to the Aum lifestyle and plunge ahead, while a part of me took a step back and watched it all with a sober eye.

So anyway, after this "Christ Initiation" I had too many doubts about Aum and I couldn't do the work I was assigned. I couldn't easily swallow the doctrine of Vajrayana [a form of tantric Buddhism]. There weren't any other followers I could express my doubts to, and the Leader was too high up for me to talk to him directly. Even if I did say to someone I thought Aum was into some questionable things, I'd just get a stereotypical response: "Mr. Takahashi, all we can do is follow Aum." I decided I had to talk to one of the leaders if I wanted to get anywhere.

While all this was going on, Mr. Niimi, Eriko Iida, and Naropa . . . asked me to see them, and as another kind of initiation they tied me up and yelled all kinds of things at me: "Why can't you follow the life we lead in Aum?" "You're neglecting your training, aren't you?" "You're not devoted to the Guru!"

Thinking this was a good opportunity, I decided to bring up some of the doubts I'd been having. "Hold on just a second here," I said. "I have a lot of problems with what's going on in our church, and that's why I can't put everything I've got into our activities." I explained what I'd been feeling and Iida said: "We all feel the same way, but the only path for us is to follow the Guru."

I took it a step further: "You don't know all that much about the Guru, so how is it you can follow him? I believe in the Guru, too, but without really knowing who he is, I can't just follow him blindly." No matter how much I pressed them, the answer was always the same: "All we can do is believe him, and follow him."

I can't tell you how disappointed I was. Someone like her . . .a Mahamudra enlightened practitioner whom everyone respected—and that's all she could say? "And you call yourself an enlightened practitioner?" I asked her. If this was all I was going to hear, then questions were a waste of time. I decided to ask my superior at the Ministry of Science and Technology, Hideo Murai, but he didn't respond at all. Total silence. My last resort would have been to ask the Leader himself. I decided to give it up and quietly devote myself to my training.

We Were Given Orders

Yoshihiro Inoue was the only person I felt spiritually close to in Aum, and I wanted to question him about all this, but he was off on some secret work and I couldn't contact him. The upshot was I spent several months in turmoil.

A year after I joined Aum, Murai ordered me to collect seismology data, but with all the uncertainty about the direction Aum was taking and the general confusion, I knew I wouldn't be able to concentrate on work. I had no idea where Aum was going, so I just asked Murai point-blank: "There seems to be a hidden side to Aum. What's your take on it?" At the time I was involved in some astrology work which put me closer to the Leader and I was able to see the daily comings and goings of the higher-ups. It was like—how should I put it?—as if their activities were all hidden behind a veil or something. The person who held the key to this hidden region was Mr. Murai, so I came right out and asked him. I couldn't say it face-to-face, so I asked him over the phone. He was silent for a while, then he said: "I'm disappointed in you." At that instant I knew that my life in Aum was over.

I don't consider Aum's crimes simply reckless behavior. Of course part of it was reckless, but there was a religious viewpoint pervading those actions. That's what I want most to learn about. Probably only Asahara and Murai can explain it fully. The other followers were mere pawns, but not these two—they gave the orders, and decided things with a clear vision of their goals. The opponent I was really struggling against, standing up alone to, was the very motives of those two people.

Most of the people arrested in the gas attack were absolutely devoted followers of the Leader who wouldn't let any doubts they might have about Aum stop them [from] doing exactly as they were told. Compared to them, Toru Toyoda [one of the members arrested for the gas attacks] could still think for himself. Whenever I voiced doubts about Aum, he'd actually give it some thought. Then he'd say, "Okay, but Hidetoshi, the world is already in Armageddon, so it's a little too late for that."

I knew Toyoda quite well, as we entered Aum around the same time; after he took vows he was promoted to the leadership overnight. He rose up that fast. That's how Aum used him. "I really don't understand all that's going on in Aum myself," he told me, "but since I'm in the leadership now, I'd better behave like a leader." When I heard this I thought: "Wow, he has it tough, too. Even worse than I do." This was still before the gas attack. I was his driver for a while. . . .

The people who carried out the crime were put in a position where they were caught off guard by the orders and couldn't escape. They'd gather in Murai's room and suddenly the leaders would broach the topic, telling them: "This is an order from the top." *An order from the top*—that was like a mantra in Aum. The people who carried out the crime were chosen from among the strongest believers. "You've been specially chosen," they were told. The leaders appealed to their sense of duty. Faith in Aum meant total devotion.

That's why I wasn't chosen to commit the crimes. I was still at the bottom of the heap and hadn't yet reached enlightenment. In other words Aum didn't trust me enough. . . .

Only One Person I Trusted

If I really search my heart I can say that if Murai had told me to do it, most likely I would have run away. However, if Yoshihiro Inoue had said to me, "Hidetoshi, this is part of salvation," and passed me the bag with the sarin in it, I would have been very perplexed. If he'd told me to come with him, I might have done so. In other words, it comes down to a question of ties between individuals.

Murai was my boss, but he was cold and too far above me. If he'd told me to do it I would have asked him why, and if he'd insisted and said, "It's a dirty job but it's for the sake of Aum and I really want you to do it," I like to think that I would have hidden my true feelings, said okay, and then, at the last minute, found a way to get out of it. Like . . . Hirose, who wavered and got off the train, I think I would have struggled over what I should do, but in the end would have found a way out.

But something about Inoue captivated me. He felt a strong sense of religious duty. If I'd seen him agonizing over the situation, I think I would have done anything to help out. He was a great influence on me. So if he'd pushed me, saying this was a mission only we could carry out, I might very well have gone along. I would have been operating on a different plane. What I mean is, in the final analysis, logic doesn't play a strong role in people's motivations. I doubt if the ones who did it were even capable of thinking logically when they were given the order to release the sarin. They didn't have the presence of mind, got caught up in events, panicked, and did what they were told. No one who had the strength to think logically about it would have carried it out. In extreme cases of guruism individuals' value systems are completely wiped out. In situations like that people just don't have the mental stamina to connect their actions with the deaths of many people.

No matter how much you resist and try to put a stop to things, the fact is that in a group like Aum your sense of Self steadily deteriorates. Things are forced on you from above and you're continually attacked for not accepting the status quo, not being devoted enough, and inevitably your spirit is broken. I was somehow able to hold out, but a lot of people who entered at the same time ended up broken. . . .

I don't think either Shoko Asahara or Hideo Murai would have been able to move me because they never opened up to me. . . .

When we went through the "Christ Initiation" I started to have serious doubts about Aum's methods. I was completely disillusioned at the gulf between believers and the Leader. . . .

I Joined to Discard the World

I placed all my faith in Inoue. I was lonely in Aum, isolated. They made me do research on astrology in the Ministry of Science and Technology, something I wasn't interested in at all. There was no way I wanted to see scientific data about the movements of the stars used for some dubious enterprise like fortune-telling. One constant theme in Aum was the desire for supernatural power, but I can't understand the mentality of people who are into that. To me, it's a complete waste of time. . . .

When I entered Aum I burned every photo album I owned. I burned my diaries. I broke up with my girlfriend. I threw everything away. . . .

When I joined Aum and took vows, I was drunk on the sense of having discarded the world, though I question whether it was actually my own will that led me to take vows. Maybe I just wanted to believe that. The gas attack brought me to my senses and I left Aum. Things I'd thought were mystical became illusions that vanished without a trace. It's like you're sleeping soundly and someone yells "Fire!" and suddenly you find yourself out on the street. That was the way it felt. I'll be grappling with these Aum incidents for the rest of my life. I don't want them to fade into the background. . . .

Gas Attacks Supposed to Purify Society

No matter what special spin Aum might put on its idea of Armageddon, I don't think it can compete with the Christian idea of the Apocalypse. It's absorbed into the Christian idea. That's why you can't really explain these Aum-related incidents by looking only at the core of what makes up Aum—namely, Buddhism and Tibetan esoteric religion. . . .

Apocalypse is not some set idea, but more of a process. After an apocalyptic vision there's always a purging or purifying process that takes place. In this sense I think the gas attack was a kind of catharsis, a psychological release of everything that had built up in Japan—the malice, the distorted consciousness we have. Not that the Aum incident got rid of everything. There's still this suppressed, viruslike apocalyptic vision that's invading society and hasn't been erased or digested.

Even if you could get rid of it at an individual level, the virus would remain on a social level. . . .

I've been trying hard to come to terms with these Aum-related incidents. I go to the trial as often as I can. But when I see and hear Asahara at the trial I feel as though he's making an idiot out of me. I get nauseated, and actually vomited once. It's a sad and dreary feeling. Sometimes I think it's not worth watching, but I still can't take my eyes off him. No matter how grotesque a figure Asahara appears, I can't just dismiss him. We should never forget that, if even for a short time, this person named Shoko Asahara functioned in the world and brought about these tragic events. Unless I overcome the "Aum Shinrikyo Incident" inside me, I'll never be able to move on.

My Soul Needed Repair

Janja Lalich

Janja Lalich is an associate professor of sociology at California State University–Chico who researches cults and extremist groups with a particular focus on gender and sexuality. Besides her academic research, she has also written popular books on how to reconstruct one's life after being in a cult. Her own experience of being in a political cult dedicated to social justice issues is expressed in this essay. Similar to other cult members, she was led by a charismatic but troubled leader who verbally abused her followers until their psyches had been broken. In this essay, she reveals not only the difficulties of being in a cult but how hard it is to leave and to repair one's inner self. Only through confronting that loss, she claims, can one's soul be repaired.

I was recruited into a cult in 1975 when I was 30 years old. The previous year I returned to the United States after having spent almost four years in exile abroad, where I lived the most serene life on an island in the Mediterranean off the coast of Spain. If someone had told me that within a year I would be deeply involved and committed to a cult, I would have laughed derisively. Not me! I was too independent, too headstrong, a lover of fun and freedom.

But there I was, new to the San Francisco Bay Area and before long cleverly recruited into a group that preached Marxism and feminism and a passion for the working class.

I was told that we would be unlike all other groups on the left because we were led by women and because our leader was brilliant and from the working class. I was told that we would not follow the political line of any other country, but that we would create our own brand of Marxism, our own

Janja Lalich, "Repairing the Soul After a Cult Experience," *CSNetwork Magazine*, Spring 1996, pp. 30–33. http://www.icsahome.com/idx_articles.htm.

proletarian feminist revolution; we would not be rigid, dogmatic, sexist, and racist. We were new and different, an elite force. We were going to make the world a better place for all people.

The reality, of course, was that our practical work had little if anything to do with working-class ideals or goals. Our leader was an incorrigible, uncontrollable megalomaniac; she was alcoholic, arbitrary, and almost always angry. Our organization, with the word democratic prominent in its name, was ultra-authoritarian, completely top down, with no real input or criticism sought or listened to. Our lives were made up of 18-hour days of busywork and denunciation sessions. Our world was harsh, barren, and unrewarding. We were committed and idealistic dreamers who were tricked into believing that such demanding conditions were necessary to transform ourselves into cadre fighters. We were instructed that we were the "uninstructed" and that we must take all guidance from our leader who knew all. We were never to question any orders or in any way contradict or confront our leader. We were taught to dread and fear the outside world, which, we were told, would shun and punish us. In fact, the shunning and punishment was rampant within; but blinded by our own belief, commitment, and fatigue, in conjunction with the group's behavior-control techniques, I and the others succumbed to the pressures and quickly learned to rationalize away any doubts or apprehensions.

I remained in that group 10 years.

I Became a Person I Did Not Know

When I got out of the cult in early 1986, I had to begin life anew. I was a decade behind in everything. Both my parents had died, and I had lost touch with former friends. I had to play catch-up, so to speak, culturally, socially, economically, emotionally, and intellectually. But most important of all, I had to repair my soul. Who am I? How could I have committed the many unkind acts while in the group? Where do I belong now? What do I believe in now? Will I ever restore my faith in myself and in others? These are the kinds of questions and dilemmas that troubled me. Over time, and most recently through my contact and work with former members of many types of cults, I've come to see that the single most uniform aspect of all cult experiences is that it touches, and usually damages, the soul, the psyche.

All cults, no matter their stripe, are a variation on a theme, for their common denominator is the use of coercive persuasion and behavior control without the knowledge of the person who is being manipulated. They manage this by targeting (and eventually attacking, disassembling, and reformulating according to the cult's desired image) a person's innermost self. They take away you and give you back a cult personality, a pseudo personality. They punish you when the old you turns up, and they reward the new you. Before you know it, you don't know who you are or how you got there; you only know (or you are trained to believe) that you have to stay there. In a cult there is only one way; cults are totalitarian, a yellow brick road to serve the leader's whims and desires, be they power, sex, or money.

When I was in my cult, I so desperately wanted to believe that I had finally found the answer. Life in our society today can be difficult, confusing, daunting, disheartening, alarming, and frightening. Someone with a glib tongue and good line can sometimes appear to offer you a solution. In my case, I was drawn in by the proposed political solution to bring about social change. For someone else, the focus may be on health, diet, psychological awareness, the environment, the stars, a spirit being, or even becoming a more successful business person. The crux is that cult leaders are adept at convincing us that what they have to offer is special, real, unique, and forever and that we wouldn't be able to survive apart from the cult. A person's sense of belief is so dear, so deep, and so powerful; ultimately it is that belief that helps bind the person to the cult. It is the glue used by the cult to make the mind manipulations stick. It is our very core, our very belief in ourself and our commitment, it is our very faith in humankind and the world that is exploited and abused and turned against us by the cults.

Learning How to Trust Again

When a person finally breaks from a cultic relationship, it is the soul, then, that is most in need of repair. When you discover one day that your guru is a fraud, that the "miracles" are no more than magic tricks, that the group's victories and accomplishments are fabrications of an internal public relations system, that your holy teacher is breaking his avowed celibacy with every young disciple, that the group's connections to people of import are nonexistent, when awarenesses such as these come upon you, you are faced with what many have called a "spiritual rape." Whether your cultic experience was religious or secular, the realization of such enormous loss and betrayal tends to cause considerable pain. As a result, afterwards, many people are prone to reject all forms of belief. In some cases, it may take years to overcome the disillusionment, and learn not only to trust in your inner self but also to believe in something again.

There is also a related difficulty: that persistent nagging feeling that you have made a mistake in leaving the group; perhaps the teachings are true and the leader is right; perhaps it is you who failed. Because cults are so clever at manipulating certain emotions and events in particular, wonder, awe, transcendence, and mystery (this is sometimes called "mystical manipulation") and because of the human desire to believe, a former cult member may grasp at some way to go on believing even after leaving the group. For this reason, many people today go from one cult to another, or go in and out of the same cultic group or relationship (known as "cult hopping").

Since every person needs something to believe in, a philosophy of life, a way of being, an organized religion, a political commitment, or a combination thereof, sorting out these matters of belief tends to be a major area of adjustment after a cultic experience.

Since a cult involvement is often an ill-fated attempt to live out some form of personal belief, the process of figuring out what to believe in once you've left the cult may be facilitated by dissecting the cult's ideological system. . . . For some, it might be useful to go back and research the spiritual or philosophical system that you were raised in or believed in prior to the cult involvement. Through this process you will be better able to assess what is real and what is not, what is useful and what is not, what is distortion and what is not. By having a basis for comparison, you will be able to question and explore areas of knowledge or belief that were no doubt systematically closed to you while in the cult. Most people who come out of a cultic experience shy away from organized religion or any kind of organized group for some time. I generally encourage people to take their time before choosing another religious affiliation or group involvement. As with any intimate relationship, trust is reciprocal and must be earned.

After a cult experience, when you wake up to face the deepest emptiness, the darkest hole, the sharpest scream of inner terror at the deception and betrayal you feel, I can only offer hope by saying that in confronting the loss, you will find the real you. And when your soul is healed, refreshed, and free of the nightmare bondage of cult lies and manipulations, the real you will find a new path, a valid path, a path to freedom and wholeness.

Chapter 3

The Impact on Families: The Dangers of Cults

My Son Was in a Cult

Ellie Brenner and Joan Reminick

This powerful story is written by Ellie Brenner, whose son joined the Unification Church, a fundamentalist Christian sect formed by the Reverend Sun Myung Moon. In her account, she reveals the despair and heartache that occurs when a parent witnesses her child change and distance himself due to being in a cult. Having just moved to New York City from the West Coast to attend art school, Josh met several members of the Unification Church who convinced him to join and subsequently facilitated a complete communication break with his mother. It wasn't until a year later that they saw each other again, despite Ms. Brenner's attempts to establish contact with her son. What is most clear from reading this story is how cults manipulate young people by isolating them from those who know them best and by feeding them information that speaks to a lack in their lives. It took five years before Josh eventually began to question the beliefs that had been instilled in him, assisted by professional counselors who helped to raise doubts in his mind about the Unification Church's inconsistencies in their belief system.

When I heard about the Heaven's Gate suicides . . . I found myself crying, overcome not only by the tragedy but also by the memories it dredged up. As I watched the grieving parents of cult members on television, it was all too easy to identify with them. I understood their sense of isolation and lack of control, the terrible knowledge that your child's will was no longer his own. I knew that my son, Josh, would have done anything for the leader of his group too. And for years, I'd lived with the uncertainty of not knowing if the young man I'd raised would ever return home.

Ellie Brenner and Joan Reminick, "Trying to Save Josh," *Good Housekeeping*, Vol. 225, July 1997, pp. 67–70.

In August 1990, Josh was 19 years old and had just transferred from art school in San Francisco to the School of Visual Arts in New York City. I was happy that he'd be closer to our home in Cambridge, MA, where we'd moved when Josh was 4, a few years after I'd divorced his father.

Josh had lined up a job in an art-supply store and was set to move into an apartment with his high school friend, Sean. A vibrant, idealistic young man, my son was the kind of kid [who was concerned] about everything from racism to oil spills to world peace.

One day in late September, I tried to call him at the apartment where he was staying with two young women before he moved in with Sean. "Sorry, Ms. Brenner," one of the girls said, "but we haven't seen Josh for days. All he told us was that he was going away to some peace seminar." I thought it was odd for Josh to just take off like that.

When I phoned again a few days later I was told that he'd returned, in the company of an older woman, and collected some of his belongings. He'd refused to answer questions and left abruptly.

Alarmed, I started calling anyone who might know his whereabouts. I was shocked when the owner of the store where Josh was to start working told me Josh had called to say he wasn't taking the job after all. Then I got frightened when I learned from Sean's stepfather that Josh had left this message on his answering machine: "I've decided not to move in with Sean," he'd said. "I'm following my dreams instead."

I called the police, but was told I couldn't file a missing person's report because I didn't know for sure that Josh was missing. To them, he was just a college kid who hadn't called home in a few weeks. At my wit's end, I hired a private investigator, who gladly took my money, but, at the end of two weeks, was as clueless as I about how to find my son.

Puzzling over My Son's Disappearance

Looking back, I can see that Josh was at an especially vulnerable point in his life. Striving hard to be independent, he was still very naive. We'd been close, but Josh had had practically no contact with his father while he was growing up. Then, just after turning 18, his dad had called him. They kept in touch briefly, but when Josh pressured his father about why he hadn't provided emotional or financial support all those years, he was ultimately rebuffed. Disillusioned, Josh had been vocal about how angry he was.

Though I didn't know his whereabouts, I did know he had gone somewhere of his own volition—and that place had something to do with a peace seminar. From those circumstances, I guessed that a group might be involved. Every odd scrap of information I'd ever heard about cults seemed to fit.

Several weeks after he'd left, a note arrived. Mom, I'm okay, Josh wrote. I love you. Don't worry; I'm following my dreams. That was all. No return address or phone number.

At least I knew he was alive. Okay, I thought, if all I can trust are my own hunches, then I'll follow them as far as I can. I went to the library and researched cults. The more I read the more I feared for Josh's safety.

I was in agony waiting to hear from him again, but there seemed little else I could do. Finally, a few days before the Thanksgiving weekend, Josh called me at the office where I work as an arts events manager.

"Hi, Mom!" he blurted. "I'm in the Moonies."

I knew that was the name given to members of Reverend Sun Myung Moon's Unification Church, and at that point I was relieved. At least now I could find out as much as possible about the group. "Josh, I'm so glad to hear from you," I practically shouted into the phone. "Where are you?" Please, I thought, please tell me, and I'll bring you home.

"I can't say," he answered.

From my research, I knew I had to be careful not to scare him off. "Why don't you join me at your grandmother's for Thanksgiving," I suggested gently, trying to cover the desperation I felt.

"I don't think I can," Josh said. "I have to ask permission." He sounded so childlike—dependent and bewildered. Then he switched gears. "Mom," he said, "you can't imagine how many interesting people I've met. Everything I'm doing now is so important."

"Josh, I'd really love to see you. Won't you come home, at least for a short visit?"

"I can't, because you might have me kidnapped," Josh replied. "You know," he added, "they've been telling me you're Satan."

I felt sick. I can't remember what I said after that, but I know I told him I loved him, and he said he loved me before hanging up. I was left reeling.

All of My Mail Was Returned

The first thing I did was call the Unification Church's headquarters in New York City, but a spokesperson denied that Josh was a member. A coworker helped me find the name of a cult education group, and I was put in touch with one of its counselors.

"You've got to get your son out right away," she told me, and gave me the name of an investigator who worked with parents of cult members. This man stationed himself outside church headquarters for a week but never saw Josh.

Over the next few months, I mailed a steady stream of letters and packages to my son, all of which were returned unopened, with no explanation. Finally, I hired a lawyer on a pro bono basis, and he contacted the legal department of the church. Shortly afterward, I received a letter from Josh.

I'm fine and I'm sure you're okay, he wrote. I'm finding new and exciting things to do creatively. . . . Know that I love you. Please show your love for me by trusting me now. . . .

After a Year, I Saw My Son

A few other short notes followed, but it wasn't until nearly a year after his disappearance—July 1991—that I finally saw him. We met in the lobby of a hotel, one of several locations for Unification Church activities. He was so gaunt, it broke my heart. I rushed to kiss and hug him, and he hugged me back. He was accompanied by a middle-aged woman whom I'll call Monica, a senior church member. Dressed in a conservative skirt and blouse, she appeared totally ordinary—except for her facial expression, which seemed masklike, at odds with what was going on.

I had a camera, and Monica took several pictures of Josh and me on a lobby couch. I also took pictures of Monica and Josh together.

We walked to a nearby Japanese restaurant. Josh seemed to be starving. I don't remember exactly what he ordered, but it was a lot.

"I wish you'd write me more," I said.

He muttered that there were some things I just couldn't understand. When I asked him about his daily activities, he went into a long ideological discussion of the church's philosophy. The old Josh had been inquisitive and forthright, but this new person had obviously been conditioned to accept the group's dogma. Moon, Josh told me, had been selected by God to finish what Christ had started. It was up to Moon to bring about world peace by uniting all religions and political systems under one order—his order. This would make the world a better place, Josh told me. Moon and his wife were the "true parents" of mankind. Monica picked up where Josh left off. He seemed to have difficulty making complete sense, and he needed her help.

I grew angry listening to them, but I decided not to argue. The last thing I wanted to do was alienate Josh. When our meeting was over, we hugged good-bye.

Later, as a goodwill gesture, I sent the pictures to Monica. That was the beginning of sporadic communications between us that made it possible for me to stay in contact with Josh.

While I waited for the occasional letter or phone call from my son, I worried that he'd become ill and not receive proper care, or that he'd be shipped to another country to work as a missionary. As I'd later learn, my fears were well-founded. Josh spent his time traveling the country in a van with eight to ten other members, selling flowers and various trinkets, often, he believed, in violation of local soliciting laws. He subsisted on a diet of hastily grabbed fast food.

How Josh Got Involved

Meanwhile, my ordinary daily life changed. If I went to the grocery store, I'd think about the foods Josh liked to eat. On the subway, I couldn't sit near children or I'd cry. In some ways, it was as though Josh were dead. Like Josh, I am an artist, and the drawings I made at the time reflected my feelings. I drew people who walked in crowds, but were isolated. I drew faces without eyes—people without individuality.

Friends would ask why I didn't seek help from my congressman or try to kidnap my son. It wasn't so simple. Since Josh, ostensibly, hadn't been coerced into joining the group, kidnapping him would be a violation of his rights—legally speaking. And I was terrified that he would cut me off completely if he learned I'd gone to the authorities.

It was nearly another whole year before I saw Josh again. He invited me to a special parents' seminar at the church's headquarters. Parents were shown to a classroom to hear a young man lecture on the evil of man and how Moon's philosophy can save civilization. Any questions that couldn't be addressed with rote responses were put off with, "We'll get to that later."

It would be much later that I'd learn from Josh that the same basic ploy had been used to recruit him. He'd been approached on the street by a friendly stranger who said she wanted him to answer a few survey questions about world peace from an organization called CARP (Collegiate Association for Research of the Principle). Josh then accepted an invitation to a lecture at a nearby office building, unaware that the woman was a member of the Unification Church and that his responses were being passed on to church leaders.

The questions had been designed to elicit a respondent's most deep-seated personal conflicts—in Josh's case, his restless transition from one school to another, from one job to the next, the alienation from his father. Miraculously—or so it appeared to Josh—the lecturer seemed to be addressing all of these concerns. "You can't commit?" he was asked. "Then make a commitment now. Change the world for the better."

Intrigued, Josh agreed to attend a weekend seminar, where he sat through long lectures, with short breaks for lunch and dinner. Not for a moment was he left by himself. Nobody mentioned Reverend Sun Myung Moon. It was only by accident that Josh stumbled upon a publication with Moon's name. By that time, he felt obliged to all the kind people around him. He had no idea of the greater commitments that would later be asked of him.

There was lots of kindness in the beginning, part of a process called love-bombing. Josh was told how wonderful he was, how his talents were welcomed. Of course, he didn't know that once a person is fully immersed in church beliefs, the love-bombing stops.

He found out soon enough. While leading the typical new member's life of traveling around and raising funds for Moon (supposedly to go to feed the hungry and to further programs for world peace), Josh told me he was frequently sent into areas where soliciting was illegal. If caught, he was told to deny any connection to the Unification Church. Once, in the Bahamas, Josh was approached in a bar by detectives who questioned him, but let him off with a warning. Instead of sympathizing with Josh, his group leader scolded him vehemently for having failed to elude authorities. This sent Josh into a depression. He still believed in Moon, but he was confused. Here he'd been told that I wasn't good for him as a mother because I was divorced and that the church stood for real family values and morality. Yet he'd been asked to lie and break the law.

I Knew Josh Would Come Home One Day

In September 1992, Josh came to my parents' house in East Meadow, NY, for a barbecue, accompanied by Monica and another female church member. He looked terrible—skinny and pale—and I almost cried. He remained defensive, unwilling to listen to anything negative about Moon. My mom had fixed some of Josh's favorite foods, including apple pie. She told Monica she hoped Josh would be able to go back to school, and Monica said she thought he would. It was bizarre: These women had all the power over my son, yet my family was trying not to offend them, while convincing them that we wanted the best for Josh.

Finally, in February 1994, Josh was permitted to visit me alone. We went to the Museum of Fine Arts in Boston, where I'd arranged for us to "run into" an old high school friend of Josh's. He seemed genuinely glad to see Hannah. A few weeks later, he sent her a note, saying how good it was to see her.

During this solo visit, I had shown Josh my recent drawings. I talked about the figures in the crowds, how isolated and imprisoned they felt. Later, I received a postcard from him saying he liked my work. "I feel the ambiguity in the figures can be resolved," he wrote. I told myself that meant that

Josh—the real Josh—knew I understood he was trapped and would be home someday.

A few months later, he came home to tell me he was leaving for Russia to recruit foreign students. I was devastated and, for the first time, cried in front of him. He left in the fall of 1994, when the political situation between Russia and Chechnya was very bad. I called church headquarters to ask if my son had any protection. He didn't. Then I called the State Department and learned he was supposed to register with the U.S. Embassy in Moscow. He never did, nor apparently did the church encourage him to. I made so many calls that leaders sent Josh home for a month to straighten out "family problems."

In his letters to me, he'd been asking about old friends—something he hadn't done before. If given the chance, I felt he might finally be ready to talk things through. Drawing on the expertise of counselors I'd met and the support of my family, I decided the time was right to try to get my son back.

Holding an Intervention

In February 1995, when he came to visit, my parents and I tried not to show our nervousness as we all sat around the kitchen table. "Josh," my mother said "you've been through a lot. This may be a good time for you to reevaluate your commitment to the church."

"I was expecting something like this," he said, "but you've got to understand that groups like mine are persecuted unjustly." That was typical Unification Church rhetoric.

"Well," my dad said, "I've asked a few people who are experts in comparative religion to come by this morning."

Josh's eyes widened, and I could see his body tense.

Almost on cue, the doorbell rang, and I opened it to greet the two "exit counselors" I'd asked to come. I'd met them before and knew they were the kind of people to put anyone at ease.

Josh got up, put on his shoes, stuffed things into his backpack, then bolted out the door. Meantime, the men walked out and headed in the opposite direction. I rushed after Josh, my heart pounding. Halfway down the block, I caught up with him. "You don't have to talk to these people," I told him. "But if you have any questions at all, why not take the time to address them now?"

He thought for a long moment. "Okay," he said finally.

We caught up with the counselors, who were already around the corner, and went to a nearby coffee shop—"neutral territory," Josh called it.

The discussion began casually, then continued on and off over the next four days in our apartment and in restaurants. The men spoke eloquently about group dynamics, how Moon had shaped history to fit his own purposes, Eastern and Western philosophies and religions, and Moon's politics. On the third day, we were joined by an ex–Unification Church member who had been higher in the hierarchy than Josh, and he pointed out inconsistencies in the church's teachings.

None of these men preached, and Josh seemed clearly thirsty for this kind of conversation. He could see they were happy and healthy even though they'd left their groups. Nothing bad had happened to them—as Josh had been warned would happen to him if he left.

Finally, I Had My Son Back

I'd always thought that when Josh decided to leave the church, it would be a dramatic moment. It didn't happen that way. He was too numb from his church experience. What he said—on February 24, 1995—was that there was enough information to make the Moon organization appear questionable, and he would do some research on his own.

With my encouragement, he decided to spend three weeks at the Wellspring Retreat Center in Albany, OH, a retreat and counseling center for former cult members run by Paul Martin, a psychologist and former member of a Bible-based movement. There, Josh spoke to others who'd been in manipulative groups and had received counseling. When he returned home, I could see that he was very angry at the church. He understood that he'd been duped. When his original recruiter called, he spoke to her in a stern voice: "No, it was my own choice, and I hope you can respect that." He never returned to the Moonies.

The counselors told me it would take about a year and a half before the old Josh was really back—and that was right. Almost immediately, though, he took charge of his diet, aware that he'd been malnourished. He's been taking vitamins and eating healthy, balanced meals. Today he looks wonderful.

My big regret is that I wasn't better educated beforehand about groups like Moon's. I believe parents and teachers must talk to their children about them. Josh and I have met young people from varied backgrounds who were as easily deceived as he was.

Both of us have put our lives back on track. Josh lives a few blocks away from me now and is attending art school in Boston. He's been seeing a lovely young woman. On my own, I've demonstrated in front of places where Moon has spoken. Josh wholeheartedly approved.

Not long ago, on my way home from the supermarket, I looked up at my apartment window. There, illuminated against the night, was Josh, sitting at my kitchen table, the way I'd imagined him countless times during those long, lonely years. I can't say when I've felt more blessed.

Seeing My Family for the First Time in Six Years

Jim Guerra

In 1975, Jim Guerra, a sophomore at Harvard University, joined a religious group and spent the next ten years in exile from his family and society. His memoir recounts the hardships he endured while being a member of a Christian fundamentalist cult run by Brother Evangelist, a preacher who instilled self-loathing and shame in his followers through a variety of techniques from fasting to sexual abstinence. Additionally, a universal technique of many cults is to cut off all ties with family and friends. In this particular excerpt, Jim is finally allowed to see his parents after more than six years of having little or no contact with them. The anger that he experienced from both of his parents surprised him, yet he continued to maintain that it was due to their own sinful natures rather than anything he had done.

It had been six-and-one-half years since I called my mom that night in April of 1976, telling her I wouldn't be coming home. At that time I had no idea I would have to wait so long before seeing my family again. I had proven myself faithful many times not to call when I had the opportunity, not to leave when I could have, and not to write when I should have. I had passed through my hometown of Washington, D.C., several times, including being thrown in jail in Alexandria where a phone call home would have spared me seventy-two hours in custody. The Word of God said to forsake all, and that included my family, those closest to me who had the greatest influence on me. I had done that amidst great anguish of soul and sense of personal loss. Deep down I wanted to explain myself, my life, my doctrine, and to part with their blessing

Jim Guerra, *From Dean's List to Dumpsters: Why I Left Harvard to Join a Cult*, Pittsburgh, PA: Dorrance Publishing Co., 2000, pp. 143–150.

and understanding. At night I dreamed they accepted what I said and even came along, city to city, hopping the freights, spreading the Gospel.

But I didn't want to visit them too soon. Because they were emotionally close, they could sway me—that is, my flesh—to renounce the path I was on. They would remember the "old man," the creature with the jovial, witty personality who had left Harvard several years ago and had been transformed into a "sober," godly follower of Jesus Christ. The old was dead and I didn't want to resurrect it. I had a new nature and I battled daily to keep it holy, unspotted from the lust and pride of this world. My parents and brothers and sisters were the ones most likely to draw out the old man and lead him into sin and possibly renounce the truth.

I began to sense that the time was coming when I would face my family. The dozens of pages of letters I wrote but never sent, the explanations of my severe and austere lifestyle, the pleading, and the comforts I tried to impart—at last I could do these face to face and clear my conscience of the guilt I felt for abandoning my family.

The summer of 1982 found me in Brooklyn, New York, again at the house we had on Nevins Street. I had spent much of the winter going from South Carolina to Georgia, and then to New York. In New York Brother Evangelist told me there was a house in D.C., and asked if it would be a trial for me to go there for awhile. I told him it would be a blessing, and I set out the next day. While I was hitching a ride by the Holland Tunnel the next day, a pickup truck going to D.C., stopped and let me ride in the open back. It was about thirty degrees outside and all I had to roll up in was a stiff tarp which he used to cover gravel. By the time we got to D.C. I was shivering uncontrollably all over, chattering like a skeleton in the wind. I walked to a house in repair on 18th Street between "S" Street and Swan, just a few blocks from Dupont Circle.

We greeted the brothers and sat in front of a fire to warm the shivers out of me. We were staying in a fire-damaged townhouse that still had no roof, but did have a door to keep people out. Brother Shor was the older brother and explained to me that the house and the one next door were being renovated and it was our duty to watch them and protect the workmen's tools. Fair enough—no roof, no rent.

I Was Told I Could Visit My Family

After I finally warmed up, I took out a map to see how close my sister's house was. My mom had given me her address when I spoke to her the year before, and to my surprise we were three blocks from her house. I hit the prayer room floor and began to pray. "Does this mean this is the time for me to visit? Is the Lord finally letting this happen?" I braced myself for another disappointment. I knew if I wanted to visit too badly I wouldn't get my way. Like the rest of God's will, it was permitted only if it wouldn't make me too happy.

A couple days later Brother Evangelist arrived and became the older brother. I cautiously approached him and asked if I could talk to him. He smiled very kindly and asked me what about, and I told him about visiting my "flesh relations." He seemed open to it and didn't say much. I continued: "Please pray with me that Yahweh's will be done because I wouldn't want to go if it weren't His will. I wouldn't want those things to happen to me that happened to other brothers that went home to visit their flesh relations. I really fear the Lord in this and wouldn't want to be given a strong delusion and fall away. I don't want to be in myself about this. I fear the Lord."

Well, my speech must have impressed him because he smiled and assured me my heart was in the right place, and that he would pray with me about it. Three months later he came to me and said, "Has the Lord shown you anything about going to see 'those people?'" (He was referring to my family.) I didn't know, so I said I was ready to go if it was God's will. He smiled and told me to be ready to go the next day.

The next morning he came to me and asked me to wait another day. He wanted to be sure the Lord was in my visit. Severely disappointed, I held back my depression and submitted myself. This was no time to act rebellious. The following morning he asked me again if I had received anything from the Lord, and I explained that the Lord rarely gave me dreams about leadings. "Do you feel led?" he asked. I wasn't sure. I'd wait another day.

Be Careful What You Tell Them

Finally, on the third day, he asked me again the same question. This time I had dreamed about my family, probably because I was thinking about them all the time. I told him I dreamed I had gone to see them and he smiled and said, "Pack up." A half hour later he came to me with specific instructions about what to say and not say to my family.

"Brother, you don't need to mention that we're staying in this house. You may want to tell them you're passing through. Or you could tell them that as Yeshua didn't have a home, neither do you; that we're not above our master who didn't have a place to lay his head."

I agreed, although I felt he was acting a little paranoid.

"Also, you don't need to mention this soul's name. We need to be as wise as serpents and as harmless as doves and awake to the warfare we're in. There are parents who have threatened to kill this soul."

In each case, "this soul" referred to himself. I knew my parents wouldn't do anything violent to Brother Evangelist, but I agreed to protect him by not saying anything.

"What should I say if they ask me who our leader is?" I queried.

"Just say you have many older brothers and that Christ is the leader of the Church." I agreed to answer that way and then requested some support. "Could Brother Shor and Brother Barnabas come with me?"

He smiled and seemed relieved. "Of course. When we're facing our flesh relations, it really helps to have some fellowship with you. You know, you aren't going to find much fellowship out there in the world." I agreed, made facial gestures that indicated total agreement and submission, and asked a final question. "Would it be okay to call them before I get on the Metro so they can meet us at the station?"

"Do you think that would be wisdom, brother? It may be more wise to call them from the last station so that they wouldn't have the time to gather police or de-programmers. If they know you're coming, it gives them more time to get the fowls together."

I felt he was being too cautious but I didn't want to risk the opportunity by questioning him at this late date. I spoke to Brother Shor and Brother Barnabas and they agreed to come with me. We prayed for safety and left to face my flesh relations for the first time in six-and-a-half years.

My Family Did Not Know Whether I Was Alive or Dead

At the last stop on the blue line I called my mother and told her where I was. Shocked, she replied, "I'll be right there." About thirty minutes later my younger brother John, whom I had not seen since he was seventeen, drove up, looking so different I hardly recognized him. He choked back tears and hugged me, telling me a lot of people were very upset at me for having disappeared for so long without contacting them. We piled into the car and set out for the thirty-minute drive to Upper Marlboro, Maryland, to our nineteenth-century tobacco farmhouse on Route 4.

John was obviously glad to see me and tried a little humor with me to lighten the tension. True to my Gospel, I remained sober and didn't laugh. When I explained my conviction against humor he looked at me with disgust and disbelief. I must really have been brainwashed; all I did was joke around when I was in the world. That was my personality. John could see I was radically different and he didn't like the change. My personality must have been submerged under the influences and teachings of the group, and I ceased to be the bubbly, fun-loving guy he had known for years.

A short while before getting home, John alluded to how badly I had hurt my mother by not contacting her. "Jim," he began, "losing you was worse than death. For years we haven't known if you were alive or dead. If we knew you were dead, we would have buried you, grieved, and gone on with our lives. If we knew you were alive, we would not have worried as much. But you left us in limbo, not knowing if you were alive or dead, and it was too hard for us to handle. Mom walked around like a zombie, blaming herself for your leaving the family. Do you know how much you hurt her?"

I knew deep in my heart that he was right, but the party line spewed forth instead. "John, I know this is hard for you to understand, but I did this to follow the Lord. He said if anyone did not forsake all that he had, including his family, he could not be his disciple. I had no choice. It was either forsake you or go to hell."

This did not sit well with John. It was still a heartless thing to do. I was beginning to dislike my own doctrine.

I Did Not Want to Feel What She Was Feeling

As we drove up the circular driveway of Old Marlboro Pike, I saw the two towering tobacco barns a few hundred feet off to the right, and remembered how, as a child, I had hit baseballs off its wooden sides and sheet metal roof. The farm looked about the same as I had remembered it, shaded by an ancient maple tree that now had hypodermics in the roots feeding it nutrients to keep it alive. I was anxious to see my mother, but didn't know what kind of reception I would receive. I quickly got out of the car and walked into the kitchen with John. The wood cook stove was still there, but the ten foot ceiling now had a rotary fan. The table against the wall was overgrown with plants, like usual, leaving little seating space unencumbered by the hanging leaves of some exotic plant hanging in your face. Mom still loved her plants.

Out of the living room a fearful, tearful woman emerged fixing her reddened eyes on my eyes, quietly welcoming me back. Mom was a bundle of contrasting emotions: hatred and love, fear and relief, anger and joy. She was glad I was home, but wanted to see if it was really me. *What kind of person had he become?* she wondered. *When should I speak my mind, or will this only drive him further away? How do I welcome him and make him feel that I care without letting on that I feel he is brainwashed and following a cult leader?*

She took my hands and rubbed them, examining them front and back. "Yes." she choked, "These are your hands. The same ones I used to rub when you were a child. They are bigger now, but they haven't changed . . . same lines, same folds, same stumpy fingers." I wanted to scorn and pull away because I thought she was being silly. "Of course they're my hands," I sort of joked. "I haven't been able to purchase another pair." Not being familiar with how to deal with another person's strong emotions, I drew back into my shell, hoping not to feel what she was feeling.

After this, she let my hands go and John took Barnabas, Shor, and me up to the bedrooms where we would be staying. When John left, I turned to them and said, "Do you see the worldly sorrow the devil is trying to put on me? Looking at my hands and comparing them to when I was a baby? This is too much!"

Shor shared how he had a hard time when he went to visit his parents a few months earlier. "I love them very much," he said. "It was really hard to see them." That was comforting, and I decided to hold my ground and be faithful to the Lord.

The Tension Between My Mother and Me Was Palpable

The next morning my mother cornered me in the kitchen and with a burst of boldness asked, "Who is your leader?" The gloves had come off at last. "We have many older brothers, but Jesus is the head of our Church," I replied. (Polly want a cracker? Awk!)

She clarified the question, but clearly she could see I was stonewalling her. "So you don't want to tell me, huh? That's what I don't like about this whole thing: too much secrecy! You can't give me an honest answer, you hide from the family for years, you won't tell us the name of the group. Need I remind you the Bible says 'They which do the truth come to the light, that they don't hide and run around secretly?' (John 3:21) Aren't we supposed to let our lights shine before men and all that stuff?"

Here was a chance for me to get back at her years of feminist leanings. "Mom, haven't you read it's not a woman's place to teach? I know what the Scripture says about those things."

She was exasperated. "Well, what about the verse, 'Honor thy father and thy mother?'" (Eph. 6:1)

"Obey your parents in the Lord," (Eph. 6:2) I retorted.

"I can see you have your verses and I have mine. But what I don't understand, Jim, is why you did this to us."

"Mom, you wouldn't understand, You're carnally minded and don't understand the things of the Spirit of God. Only God can open your eyes and show you the truth." That finished the conversation.

Later I saw her on the porch looking though her binoculars at the varieties of birds that frequented the garden behind the woodshed. She had her Audubon Society bird books out trying to identify some new species that she had never seen before. Brother Shor sat with her and participated in the bird-watching, enjoying the exercise with her, subtly looking for opportunities to witness to her.

I came up to her as she sat there trying to get her mind off the monster I had become. "Jim," she invited, "come and look at these birds with us." Not being thrilled with birds since my childhood, I certainly didn't admire them in my adulthood. I reluctantly took a seat next to her on the porch and looked through the binoculars. It was great to be focused for once as I saw the clear outlines of the barn, the highway behind it, and the electric wires that ran from the shed to the well. Nevertheless, this gave us an opportunity to speak.

"Do you see that one with the pretty yellow tail and the red stripe on its wing?" she asked.

"Naw," I said, hoping the subject would change. "I remember one time I was camped in California and found a pretty shell. When I showed it to the older brother he reminded me that we should be careful not to worship the creation more than the Creator."

Again I had alienated her by misusing a Scripture. She was then convinced I didn't have both oars in the water and she didn't like the person I had become.

My Dad Asked Whether I Was Happy

That night, immediately after I called my father who lived about forty-five minutes away, he came over to see me. He was gentle and very loving, not condemning me at all. He had grayed considerably and was slightly bent over with age, not the robust man I had remembered from 1976. He gave me a long hug and we sat down on the steps to talk.

"So, how are you doing, son?"

"Fine, Dad."

"Are you happy with what you're doing?"

"Yes."

"Really? Are you really happy, son?"

I thought back on the time I had spent in the group and, except for the pain of leaving the family and being celibate, life was all right. "Yes, Dad, I am happy."

"Do you miss us?"

"Yes, I do."

"Are you allowed to write?"

"Yes." It was a half-truth. I could write if I didn't mind the stigma of being suspected of being unfaithful.

"I have been worried about you, son. Did you ever break into my house in Rockville one summer when I wasn't there?"

I was shocked by the question. "Why would you ask that?"

"Well, when you don't hear from someone for a long time, you begin to imagine funny things. While you were gone, someone broke into the house in Rockville, climbed through the basement window, ate some food, watched some TV, and then left, without taking anything. It has haunted me for years. We thought maybe you had come and dropped in and left."

"No," I said. "That wasn't me."

"I told myself if I ever saw you alive again I would ask you that question. I'm just so glad to see you that you can't imagine. Your sister, Catherine, thought she saw you on an on-ramp in Connecticut or somewhere when she went on vacation. When she turned around to come and get you, the person was no longer there. She cried for a long time after that."

I Tried Not to Let on That Anything Was Wrong

By now I was getting the message. My disappearance and silence over the years had hurt them deeply, and they couldn't imagine why I was behaving this way.

"I used to come down to Dupont Circle every weekend for about two years to look for you. I think I met some of your buddies, but I didn't bother asking them about you because I knew they wouldn't tell me anything," he chuckled. "Would they?" he asked.

"No," I agreed. "They wouldn't have told you anything."

"That's what I thought," he replied. "Well, son, are you sure you are doing what you want to be doing with a free will?"

"Yes, Dad. I'm doing what I want to be doing with my own free will." At the time I didn't realize the way I was being manipulated and how trapped I was [in]to the group's doctrine and fear tactics. I believed that leaving the group would destroy me spiritually forever.

"Can you write from time to time to let us know how you are doing?"

"I'll try. We aren't allowed to send mail from any cities that we are in, but I can write to you when I am on the road."

"Why is that? Is it a security precaution?" I was amazed at how insightful my father was. He seemed to see through the group better than I did.

"Yes. We have had problems in the past with parents of members of the group persecuting us."

"Don't you think maybe you brought this on yourself by disappearing and not contacting the families? Perhaps if you kept in contact with the families you wouldn't have so much persecution!"

That made perfect sense to me, and I remember having thought it when I first learned about the secrecy of the group.

He asked me a few more questions about how I lived and how we provided for ourselves, and he was mildly amused at the ingenuity and the survival skills I had acquired. Then he hit me below the belt.

"Do you think you'll ever get married?"

"I'd like to."

"Does the leader permit marriages?"

"Yes, some."

"Isn't it hard for you to be alone and not have a mate?"

"It is difficult, but God gives me the grace." That answer satisfied my doctrinal side, but did nothing for my testosterone level.

"I want grandkids!" he bellowed in jest, with a big smile.

I'd love to make you some, I thought to myself. I was really troubled about the strictness of Brother Evangelist's marriage policy, allowing only one marriage in six-and-a-half years, but I didn't want to let on that there was anything wrong with the Church. I was there to convert them as much as I was there to appease my own conscience.

We parted on good terms and he invited me over to see his new family the next day. I told him I would like to, and when Brother Evangelist called the next day he told me to be careful.

My Emotions Finally Could Not Be Contained

On the drive over, my father began to vent his real frustration and anger about my leaving the family and not contacting them. I was surprised and became very defensive. I felt like getting out of the car and almost asked him to let me out on Interstate 95. He finally settled down as we arrived in Rockville, and we avoided any further conflict that day.

On the final day of the visit, Brother Evangelist called and told me to pack up and return to the house on Nevins Street in New York City. I was ready to go. Emotionally, I was drained and could take no more confrontation. Brother Barnabas accompanied me as I walked around the farm one last time before leaving it. Behind the toolshed I began to weep openly for them, consciously telling myself I was weeping for their lost, sinful state, but really weeping because I was ashamed and sorry for how much I had hurt them and how much they loved me.

I hadn't realized how much I had hurt them until this visit, nor did I realize how much they loved me. But instead of facing these realities, the religious beast within me swallowed up the pain and renamed it "Godly sorrow for sinking sinners." Shor tried to comfort me, relating to me his visit home. "It does strange things to you," he said. "You think you're going to be strong, but you are never really ready for what emotions you meet when you go to visit your family." That was so true.

My Father Tried to Help Me Leave Scientology

Anonymous

Started by the science fiction writer, L. Ron Hubbard, Scientology is well known as an established spiritual movement with many celebrities, such as actors Tom Cruise and John Travolta and the singer Beck, claiming membership. Viewed in its most positive light, Scientology is a set of teachings and philosophies that lead its members to a higher sense of well-being through the uncovering of repressed memories and traumas over the course of a number of lifetimes the individuals might have experienced. Scientology's most dominant practice is one-on-one counseling, also known as "auditing," which is a practice used to generate information from members, also known as preclears, to discover what issues they most need to address. Some of the techniques to help members relieve themselves of their emotional baggage, however, have been harshly criticized.

In this essay, the writer discusses one of the more controversial practices, known as "disconnection," in which preclears are told to cut off all connections with friends and family members who appear to be antagonistic toward Scientology. In a conversation with her father, the writer realizes that her father is trying to convince her to leave Scientology despite her objections. Telling her counselor leads to categorizing the writer's father as an SP—a suppressed person—who is not supportive of his daughter's decision to be a Scientologist. After breaking off all connections with her family, the writer realizes that she has now become "a real Scientologist."

"Your mother and I have been reading about this Scientology," he told me. He took some newspaper clippings from his briefcase. "Here. I want you to read these."

Anonymous, "Told to Disconnect from Her Parents," *The Road to Xenu*, FACTNet BBS, 1993. http://www.culthelp.info.

I picked up one of the clippings. It was from *Time* Magazine. The writer was obviously biased against Scientology. In the article Scientology was called a cult.

"Scientology's not a cult," I informed my father. "It's just a group of people trying to make a difference in the world. This writer obviously didn't talk to anyone in Scientology or he wouldn't have written these things." I handed the article back to him.

"Well, there are other articles," he handed me several other articles. I looked through them. The orientation of the writers was obvious.

"Dad, this is just entheta," I told him, remembering what Hubbard had taught about this kind of journalism on one of his tapes. "That means it is against theta, or goodness. We're not supposed to read this stuff," I told him coldly, pushing the article back to his side of the table.

"But just read some of them," he pleaded with me.

"I don't need to read them. I know what they say without reading them. They are written by the suppressive press. These writers are paid by their bosses to write this stuff. They want to destroy Scientology because it works.

"There are vested interests in this country who don't want to see Scientology expand. It is a threat to them because they want to enslave people and Scientology is in the business of freeing people." Out of my mouth were coming the phrases I had heard over and over on Hubbard's training tapes.

My Dad Was a Suppressive Person

"You are in a dangerous cult," my father argued with me. "We want you to quit this foolishness and come home. That's why I am here. I have come to get you and to take you home."

I looked at my dad with disbelief. He was beginning to sound like a Suppressive Person. A very unpleasant thought began to form in my mind.

Could it be possible that my dad was an SP? "How does mom feel about this?" I asked him.

"She totally agrees. We both want you home. You can go back to the university. If you come back now, you can still enroll for the spring semester." He was looking at me hopefully.

"I don't want to come back. I don't want to go back to school. This is where I belong. I have a job here. I am helping to clear the planet. There is nothing on this whole planet more important than Scientology. These writers are wrong about Scientology. Scientology is the only hope on this planet that any of us have." I was beginning to get desperate. Could my father force me to go back with him?

"No, you are wrong," my father said, beginning to sound angry. "This Scientology is nonsense. You are in a cult. And I am going to take you home. I want you to get your things and come with me. I have a ticket for you to come back with me to Michigan." He pulled the ticket from his pocket. It was made out in my name.

I started to cry. "Dad, I can't come back with you. I don't care what you think about Scientology, you just don't understand. You can't tell me what to do anymore. I'm eighteen. Scientology is my life. I've signed a contract to work here and I'm not leaving."

"What kind of contract?" he asked suspiciously.

"A Sea Org contract. I signed a contract to work for the Sea Org for a billion years. We're going to clear the planet. Then we're going to clear all the other planets in the universe. Scientology is the first chance in millions of years for us to be free. And I'm not going to mess it up. There's nothing in the world out there that I want to do. How could I go back to music school when I have a chance here to help with something really important?"

He looked at me with a combination of exasperation and disbelief. "How can I get you to see the truth about what you are involved in?" he asked me. "Can't you see the absurdity of what you are saying? Clearing the planet? This is nonsense. You need to come to your senses." Now he was really sounding angry.

"Dad, I'm not coming back with you. I'll have dinner with you and talk to you, but I'm not coming back to Michigan. And you can't make me." I was not about to give in.

He stared helplessly out the window. Then he turned to me and started speaking in a kinder, less angry voice.

I Was Not Going to Leave

"Look, I know we have never shown much affection in our family. But you know that we love you. We care about you. Why do you think I came all the way out here to see you? We all care. Your brothers and sisters miss you too. We all want you back home."

"And what will you do if I don't come?" I asked him.

"We'll try something to get you back. Legally. We'll fight. We'll sue this cult if we have to. We're not going to give up to some harebrained cult," he threatened.

Now I knew the truth. My father was an SP. Hubbard had made it clear. I had read all the teaching on the Suppressive Person on the course. The basic crime of the Suppressive Person was to attack Scientology, the only force for good and reason on the planet.

I had read about this in the Ethics book. The Suppressive Person was also called the "anti-social personality," or the "anti-Scientologist." "There are certain characteristics and mental attitudes which cause about 20% of a race to oppose violently any betterment activity or group," Hubbard had written. Such people, he said, cause untold trouble for betterment groups such as Scientology. "The anti-social personality supports only destructive groups and rages against and attacks any constructive or betterment group." Of course, I thought. My father works for the government. According to Hubbard, the government is completely suppressive. I had listened to tapes where he had told us all about the suppressive agencies in the federal government: the IRS, the FDA, the FBI, the National Institute for Mental Health. The government, explained Hubbard, was a suppressive organization that controlled this country. But the real truth was that behind this government was an invisible government that most people didn't know about. It consisted of a secret group of twelve extremely powerful men who were the real source of power in the world. They were particularly connected with the World Health Organization in Europe. And they pulled the strings that ran this country. And the people who worked for the government, like my father, were just minor suppressives that were attracted to this kind of work because it was consistent with their real inner evil natures.

I stared at my father with amazement. My eyes were being opened. Now I understood why there had been so much trouble in our family. My father was, as Hubbard put it, a "blazing SP."

"Look, I'm not coming home. And I don't want you to cause any trouble for Scientology. That would just get us both in trouble." I looked at him coldly. I got up from the table. "I'm going back to the center. I can't stay here with you. I'm sorry you wasted your trip but you did that on your own determinism, and I can't take responsibility for it (more Scientology-talk)."

I walked out the door, not looking back at him.

I Was Told to Disconnect from My Family

I ran back to the center, and burst into Aileen's office. "Aileen, my dad is threatening to sue Scientology. He says it's a cult. He wanted me to go back home with him," I said, obviously upset.

She looked at me, concerned. "Why? What happened? Tell me exactly what happened and what he said."

I related the whole event to her. She looked troubled.

"I'm afraid I'll have to write up a knowledge report about this," she told me. "It seems that your father could be a source of trouble for us. You'll have to work this out with Ethics. And until its handled, I'm afraid you won't be able to go back on course. But the first thing that you need to do is to go and report everything that has happened to the MAA [Master at Arms]."

She pulled a routing form out of her top drawer. At the top it said, "Ethics Routing Form."

Several minutes later, I sat in the chair opposite the teenage Ethics Officer, telling him the same story I had told Aileen.

"I would like to indicate that your father is a Suppressive Person," he looked across the desk at me as if I were infected with a deadly virus, "and the policy on suppressives is very clear." He handed me a policy letter written by Hubbard. I read through it carefully. The policy on suppressives, according to Hubbard, was to "handle" or "disconnect."

"What does that mean?" I asked the young boy sitting across from me. Wrong question. "What word don't you understand?" he looked at me with emotionless eyes.

"I understand the words. I just don't understand what I'm supposed to do," I said.

"Very simple. Either you handle your father. That means to the point where he is willing that you continue in the Sea Org, or you will have to disconnect from him. You will have to send him a disconnect letter."

"Disconnect letter?" It sounded ominous.

"Yes. I can help you write it. You will tell him that you want no contact with him or with the rest of your family now or at any point in the future. You will formally disconnect from your suppressive family. And until you handle the situation in one way or the other, you won't be allowed back on course. That's policy. I'm going to give you twenty four hours to make your decision. You are to report back to me at this same time tomorrow." The policy, I realized, was black and white. Like everything else in Scientology. There was no room for feeling. Not that I minded the lack of emotion with which this and similar situations were handled in Scientology. I had already done enough to not feel much about anything. But to tell your parents goodbye forever . . . I squirmed inwardly at the thought. Yet I believed in the policy. I was already conditioned to believe that if Hubbard said it, it must be right. I knew that Hubbard's way would always be the best and most rational solution because he was "Source." In just a few short weeks, Hubbard had already assumed occupancy of the place in my mind allocated to Father, or Dad. He loved me, I believed, even more than my own father did. He was father to us all.

I walked back to the house, having been barred from the course until this problem was resolved. I thought of my dad. He'll be home in a couple of hours, I thought. I'll call him and maybe he'll be more reasonable. Maybe he can be "handled."

My Father Fit the Bill for an SP

But in my mind the decision had already been made. My father had taken on the color of the enemy. I no longer thought of him as father. All these years, I thought, I had been living with an SP and not known it. This explained all the conflict in my family. And by virtue of being married to an SP, my mother was by (Scientology) definition a "PTS," or Potential Trouble Source. And both of them were now endangering my Scientology career.

If they didn't agree to back off, I thought, I will have to disconnect. I have to get back on course. Already my stats for the week are crashed, I thought dismally, wondering what ethics condition I would be assigned for the week.

I lay on my bed, thinking back over all the years with my father. I thought of the twelve characteristics Hubbard lists in the Ethics book as being characteristic of an SP.

"1. He or she speaks only in broad generalities." Yeah, I thought, my dad is always talking about "they this" and "they that."

"2. Such a person deals mainly in bad news, critical remarks, invalidation and general suppression." Bulls eye, I thought. My father had a definite tendency to be critical. I thought of all the times he came home complaining about his co-workers, criticizing what they had done during the day.

"3. The anti-social personality alters, to worsen communication . . . passes on 'bad news.'" Again I thought of times when my dad told us less than flattering stories about the "imbeciles" he worked with.

"4. He does not respond to treatment or psychotherapy." Once, I remembered, my mother had tried to get my dad into counseling to work on their marriage and he refused to go.

"5. Surrounding such a personality we find cowed or ill associates or friends who, when not driven actually insane, are yet behaving in a crippled manner in life, failing, not succeeding." My mother is always sick, I thought, and what about my problems. And my sister is always having trouble in school. I didn't need to read any further. There was no doubt in my mind. My dad was an SP. And now he was trying to interfere with me trying to help Scientology clear the planet. I began to feel angry. I'm not going to let him do this to me, I thought. I'm going to get ethics in on my family. If I have to disconnect, then that's what I'll do.

I Couldn't Imagine Life Without Mom and Dad

I waited for the hours to pass. I was dreading the call. Finally I walked down to the convenience store a couple of blocks away and placed the call. My mother answered the phone. She sounded cheerful. "Hi, dear. We were just thinking about you."

"Is dad there?" I asked her coldly. I knew what I was up against. My mother had no idea of the situation she was in, that she was a PTS to a deadly SP. "Yes, he just got in. I'm so disappointed that you didn't come back with him. But you need to know that we love you and we'll always be here for you." "Could I just talk to dad?"

He came on the line. "Margery, we're not going to give up without a fight. You tell Scientology that they will hear from my lawyer. I'm not going to stand for this nonsense."

"OK, dad. I'm sorry you feel that way. Tell mom goodbye for me," I said, then quickly hung up the phone.

There's no going back now, I thought. I went back to the house and spent a sleepless night tossing to and fro, my sleep haunted with nightmares about my father. In one dream, he had a gun and was standing outside the center shooting through the windows.

The next morning I walked over to the center and went directly to the Ethics office.

"I need to disconnect from my family," I stated calmly. "There's no hope of ever dealing rationally with my father. He's insane on the subject of Scientology. Hubbard was sure right about SP's. They hate what we are doing to save this planet."

"So what do I have to do?" I looked across at the teenage Master at Arms. "Here's what you have to write," he replied, handing me a blank sheet of paper and a pen. He began to dictate. "I am writing to notify you that I hereby disconnect from you." He paused as I wrote. "I want no further contact with you at any time or under any circumstances. This decision is irrevocable." I wrote down exactly what he said. "Now sign it," he commanded. Then he handed me an envelope. "You can make this out and we will mail it for you."

I addressed the envelope.

"That's all there is to it," he said matter of factly. "I will give you a form to get you back on course. You're going to have to push to get your stats back up."

"I know," I answered. "But I'll do it. Thursday is still three days away." I walked back to the courseroom. Just like that, I thought. I tried to comprehend the fact that I would never see or write to my parents ever again. Somehow, it didn't seem real. I couldn't quite imagine life without mom and dad to fall back on.

"Well, I guess I'm on my own now," I thought. "I know I did the right thing. I just wish I felt better about it."

For a moment I had a fleeting thought to run back up the street to the store to call my dad and ask him for the ticket back home.

But I quickly pushed the thought from my mind. "Family," I thought to myself, "is the second dynamic. The Sea Org is the third dynamic." Then I repeated to myself the phrase I was to hear many times in the coming years. "The greatest good for the greatest number of dynamics," I thought. "Scientology must survive. My relationship with my family is not important. All that is important is clearing the planet."

Scientology Is My Family

I can't think about them anymore, I told myself as I approached the center. They are no longer my family. Scientology is my family. And this is my real home.

I walked resolutely into the courseroom. I was more determined than ever to do well in Scientology.

I didn't think about my family again for a long time. I read the letters from my mother that would arrive periodically at the center, but I would throw them in the trash, feeling no emotion whatsoever.

I had passed my first initiation.

I was now a real Scientologist.

They Convinced Me That My Parents Were Satanists

Brittany Morgan and Laura Billings

While cults are often thought to be linked to fringe religious or political movements, there are some that promote new forms of therapy that are manipulative and dangerous. One such cult, which Brittany Morgan, the author of the following viewpoint, calls simply The Group, based its philosophy on a twelve-step model similar to Alcoholics Anonymous in which extreme techniques are used for confronting difficult issues and uncovering repressed memories. Morgan was attracted to this therapy because of its "quick fix" techniques that shortened the therapeutic process. Once a member of The Group, however, the author was subjected to horrifying experiences that involved anger therapy, which often led to flashbacks and blackouts. It was during a five-day workshop that Morgan had a flashback in which she realized her parents were members of a satanic cult who had sexually abused her. Encouraged by the two leaders of The Group, whom Morgan calls Mary and Margaret, Morgan cut off all ties with her parents for two years, substituting The Group for her family. During one of these so-called therapy sessions to uncover hidden memories, however, Morgan fell into a catatonic state that led to her being admitted to a psychiatric hospital. Eventually, she was saved by an ethical therapist who helped her reunite with her parents. Along with other plaintiffs, Morgan sued Mary and Margaret for malpractice. The case was settled out of court.

I saw Mary and Margaret for the last time at a fast-food place on the outskirts of town. They told me that meeting at their office as we usually did would put them and everyone

I loved in jeopardy, and in the state I was in, I believed them. They told me that if I didn't leave town immediately, my parents would soon find me and take me back to their satanic cult. They urged me to get as far away as I could, to change my name and face as soon as I got there. I felt like I was losing my world, but the two women I'd come to think of as surrogate parents were firm, insistent. If I did as they told me and went underground, they promised, there might be a chance I could come back to them someday. I wrote out a last will and testament that entrusted them with my journals and my few possessions. Then they asked me to sign a disclaimer saying that if I ever accused them of wrongdoing, it would be because I'd fallen back into my family's cult. I signed it willingly. Mary and Margaret were my therapists, and I trusted them with my life.

It's several years later now, and I'm in my late twenties and living in a different city; and although I came here to disappear, I've found myself instead. In the years I've spent trying to piece together the broken parts of my life, I've come to understand that I really was once a member of a cult—a psychotherapy cult built around the two women I'm calling Mary and Margaret (their names, like all those in this article, including mine, have been changed). The story I'm about to tell is not about how psychotherapy ruined my life. It's true that bad therapy set me back, took years from my life and left me with more questions than answers. But it's also true that good therapy, with an ethical, honest, professional counselor, has helped me to get my life back. Maybe if you read my story, you'll know better than I once did how to tell the difference.

When I look back on my childhood, I think of myself as a weird little kid—a lonely child who never quite fit in at school and a confessor for my parents, each of whom confided too much to me about their troubled marriage. I spent most of my childhood in fear of my father's rage, trying to stay out of range of his outbursts. I hid my own emotions—but when I moved away from my parents to go to college, all those bottled [up] feelings of anger and terror began to emerge. I couldn't face them. I started drinking a lot. I stopped eating, and when I couldn't keep that up, I started bingeing and purging.

Then a friend told me about a therapy group she was in that I'll call The Group. It was run by two women counselors with apparently good credentials and a comfortable office in a sleepy suburb. A lot of their philosophy was based on the 12-step model of groups like Alcoholics Anonymous, but what really appealed to me was their belief that therapy didn't have to be a five- or six-year commitment. When I met them, Mary and Margaret explained that they believed in accelerating the process by pushing patients to confront difficult issues almost continually, so that they could be "cured" in just two or three years. It seemed empowering to be able to take such control in solving my problems, so I called my parents and asked if they would pay for my therapy sessions. At first, my father said absolutely not. But my mom, who knew how much I was struggling, convinced him. Within a week, I started individual therapy with Mary (the clients were assigned individual sessions with either Mary or Margaret), as well as occasional evening group therapy classes on such topics as sexuality, love, family dynamics and relationships. The drive from my campus took more than an hour each way, but I was happy to do it. I felt like I was finally doing something good for myself.

Unleashing a Lifetime of Suppressed Rage

Within a month, Mary said I was ready for my first "anger session." You've probably heard about how, for some people, hitting a pillow or screaming at a stand-in for your parents can be a way of releasing suppressed anger. Still, no textbook could have prepared me for what I saw that day. There were about 30 of us gathered in the office basement. The lights were down and the therapists started playing some slow music with sad lyrics that made many people start to cry. Then we broke into smaller "anger areas," where we sat in a circle. I sat with my back to the corner, thinking I'd be safer there. But then the man next to me grabbed an oversize wiffle bat at the center of the circle and started pounding a big pillow with a loud, persistent Thwack! Thwack! Thwack! just a couple of feet from where I sat. He was a big man, maybe 6'3", and as he continued pounding, others in the circle shouted out to provoke him. Amid their deafening shouts, his rageful screams turned to mournful howls. Everyone in the room was screaming, shouting, crying—so much raw energy that I could feel every heartbeat in my throat. I was horrified—and yet, when it was my turn, I picked up the bat. I felt awkward at first, and so self-conscious I don't know if I even made a sound. Gradually, I overcame my discomfort—so much so that, at the anger sessions I attended several times a year, I actually looked forward to the cathartic feeling of going out of control.

Since most of us were in group therapy together, everyone knew what everyone else's issues were. For instance, if you were overweight, someone in the group might shout out, "You're so fat no one could love you!" Or, if you were an incest survivor, one of the therapists might say, "You want to be Daddy's little whore?" The person in the center of the circle would get more enraged, more rattled, until often he or she would experience flashbacks—memories of painful experiences that somehow felt real and present again.

We Were Fine—Society Was Sick

I never questioned whether this provoking of hopped-up emotion could actually be "good" for people, or whether it might be considered unethical, or even abusive. For one thing, I was really impressed by the other people in The Group. They were older than I was, smart, well educated and affluent. Most lived in expensive, old-money neighborhoods, and many had Ph.D.'s. I found it thrilling to be in discussions with people who were so articulate, so intelligent. If they thought this was okay, why shouldn't I?

Another reason I never questioned The Group's methods was that such questioning really wasn't tolerated. Mary and Margaret believed that our society and everyone in it were damaged and unhealthy. They believed that addiction was rampant, and that you could be addicted to everything from magazines to your own children. If you expressed any sort of discomfort with their methods or rules, Mary and Margaret said it was simply because you, too, were a victim of our sick culture. So if you questioned the point of an "anger session" or challenged their rule against taking aspirin, Mary's and Margaret's response would be that you, too, were "in the disease." Having lived through an experience as intense as an anger session, and having bonded with these people in a way I never had with my own family, I simply couldn't risk alienating them. I had finally found a place where I felt accepted for who I was, rage and all. Going to therapy felt like I was finally coming home.

"Detaching" from Mom and Dad

Within three months, the pace of the therapy sessions had accelerated. I was in a weekly class, a weekly individual session and a weekly support group, all while keeping a full schedule at school. As The Group's rules required, I stopped drinking caffeine, taking aspirin, eating sugar or using any other substance that might tamp down my true emotions. When friends worried that The Group was taking too much control of my life, I told them they were "in the disease." When Mary suggested that I was ready for the next stage—"detaching" from my parents—I was willing.

Mary and Margaret met with my parents and told them I could work through my issues more quickly if I cut off all contact with them for two years. My parents and I screamed and argued, but in a final, tearful conversation with my mother, I was able to convince her how much this mattered to me. I sent letters to my relatives that year in my Christmas cards, explaining why I wouldn't be seeing them anymore. When I look back, cutting them off so harshly is one of the mistakes I regret most.

Still I was making progress, and I was making friends in The Group. In anger sessions, I was experiencing many flashbacks. At first, these memories were the familiar ones from childhood, but emotionally charged—as if I were experiencing all the rage and shame I should have felt as a kid watching my parents fight, or being yelled at for some small mistake. Mary and Margaret pushed us into confronting these buried issues with an almost relentless zeal.

The more memories we dredged up, the more praise we got, the more we were "progressing." What I didn't know then was that most therapists would never encourage this exhausting pace. Constantly coping with these issues—on top of being a full-time student—was wearing me down.

Bizarre "Flashbacks" from the Past

Two months after cutting off contact with the parents, I went to an intensive five-day workshop where I had the most awful flashback yet. The workshop was held at an old church camp. On the second or third day, I walked into the sanctuary, saw the altar and suddenly dropped to my knees. It was like a scene from a science-fiction movie where you're jolted into the past. I saw myself as a young girl, being sold to two men who abused me sexually in some sort of ritual. I sobbed violently for hours afterward. This horrifying memory felt real to me. And yet, no matter how bizarre my flashbacks were (or anyone else's—many Group members "remembered" being abused in satanic rituals), The Group never challenged or questioned them. If you didn't believe them, you were simply "in the disease." By examining my flashbacks with The Group, I came to believe that they were real, and that my parents were members of a satanic cult. I moved off-campus into an apartment with a fellow Group member to make it harder for my parents to find me. They were the enemy and I never wanted to see them again.

You might think this discovery would have uprooted me, but, in fact, I felt I'd found a better family. I thrived on the feeling of belonging I had in The Group. When I got a positive stroke from Mary and Margaret, I'd be flying. But if I made a complaint—if I worried that I couldn't keep up with my classes and all the therapy groups they wanted me in, much less pay for them—they would shun me and tell me I was "in the disease."

We all craved their approval so much that no demand they made seemed too burdensome or too silly. If Mary and Margaret told you that you were "addicted" to reading the newspaper and eating apples, then you would quit reading the newspaper and eating apples. If you had sexual thoughts about someone in The Group, you were supposed to tell that person in order to get the sexual feelings "out of the way" of your therapy. You had to get Mary's and Margaret's permission to begin a romantic relationship. Some married couples weren't even supposed to have sex unless Mary and Margaret approved it. Few of us objected. Most of us had cut off every relationship we had with the outside world. Mary and Margaret and The Group were all we had, and we'd do anything for them.

Going Off the Deep End

About a year after I'd experienced my first horrifying flashback, the rapid-fire pace of these sex-abuse memories started to slow down. My therapists told me it was because I was holding onto something deep and buried—and they began suggesting possibilities. I would kneel in the center of the group circle and begin hitting the pillow. "How do you feel?" the therapists would ask. "Angry," I'd respond. "Who's there with you?" they'd ask. "I don't know," I'd say. Soon they would offer examples—"Is it your uncle? What is he doing to you?"—

and a hazy picture would form in my mind. These flashbacks had such a dark tone, and I began to "remember" scenes of abuse and terror at the hands of my parents and family friends. The process felt very different from the way I had dredged up memories before. Now, rather than having a memory that helped me understand my real feelings, I was having a feeling and then trying to match it to a "memory"—trying to figure out something that might not even be there. It was sort of like watching a scary movie and not knowing what's going to pop out of the corner until someone says "a guy with a knife"—then your imagination takes you there. Unlike my earlier memories, which were clear and chronological, these were murky. Even so, I really believed what my therapists told me: that this was a technique for getting at deeper issues and that it would help me get better.

When the two-year detachment period my parents had promised was up, they contacted Mary and Margaret and demanded to see me, to know where I was living. At this point, my progress in therapy was slowing down because I refused to confront a very troubling flashback that Mary and Margaret were convinced was the key to my getting better. At a group session one night, Mary and Margaret demanded that I "go into" this flashback, so I lay on the floor and started flailing my arms and legs, a tantrum technique we sometimes used to take us into a trance-like state. I kicked and screamed so much that I seemed to lose touch with my body. I fell into a catatonic state in which I couldn't speak or respond. The ambulance came for me five hours later, at 2:00 A.M., and that morning I woke up in a hospital psychiatric ward. The resident psychiatrist tried to understand what had brought me there, but I called Mary and Margaret, who warned me to be careful about what I said, because other mental-health professionals might be "in the disease," too. I was hospitalized for five weeks.

Forced to Live a Brand-new Life in the Underground

I thought Mary and Margaret wanted me to get better, but now I believe they wanted me out of the way. I was volatile and fragile, my parents were calling constantly and, I later learned, my parents' lawyer had hired a private detective to find me. My crisis had attracted too much attention. The police wanted to know what sort of therapeutic practice had sent me to the ER in the middle of the night. I guess I had become a liability. So Mary and Margaret told me to leave town, and a member of The Group came to my house (I'd just been released from the hospital) with $3,000 in cash so I could escape the satanic cult they said was pursuing me. I believed I was in danger. More important, I knew that if I didn't follow their instructions, I'd never be allowed to come back. I did what they asked.

The first weeks of my exile were a blur. I stayed with a Christian family who were part of an underground network to help satanic-cult survivors. At Mary's insistence, I legally changed my name, had a nose job, changed my hair color, got colored contact lenses and bought new clothes in a completely different style. I even changed the way I walked. I was alone in a place where everything was different—the air, the time zone, the people—and where I had no roots, no friends, no one to talk to. When I looked in the mirror, I had no idea who I was.

Before I left, Mary and Margaret had encouraged me to continue with my therapy through an organization that helped survivors of satanic cults. (At the time, it never occurred to me that it was, in fact, therapy that had brought me to this point.) When I went to see my very patient new therapist, she must have known immediately that the treatment I'd received with The Group was unethical. Yet she knew that challenging my fierce loyalty to them would send me out the door. I came to her office one night with a letter I'd just gotten from Mary and Margaret. I was too scared to read it alone. It was shattering. They wrote that they knew I'd gone back to the satanic cult, that I was a sick person who would never be allowed back into The Group, that the belongings I'd asked to have sent to me had been destroyed in a basement flood. I sobbed when I read it. I felt completely alone. I excused myself to go to the bathroom, but instead walked out to the top floor of the parking structure and climbed over the railing. I had done everything they asked, and yet they would never take me back. I had felt suicidal before, but I had never come as close as this. My therapist found me as I was contemplating my leap and said, "Don't do this now in front of me." She told me that she cared about me and didn't want to lose me. It was the right thing to say, because even though I had only known her a short time, I didn't want to hurt her by hurting myself. Together, we went back inside. That night was a turning point for me. Although part of me still hoped that I could one day win Mary's and Margaret's approval again, I had finally started to understand that I had to live life for myself.

Facing the Cult Leaders in Court

A few years later, I sat in the conference room of a lawyer's office. Across from me were Mary and Margaret, surrounded by their own lawyers. This had become a fairly common setting for them—I was one of more than a dozen ex-Group members suing the two therapists for malpractice. It had taken me a long time to come to this decision.

I had slowly reestablished contact with some of my friends who had left The Group. They told me they had come to believe that The Group was actually a cult. They gave me a book that contained a checklist of cult characteristics. A cult, it said, is a group that holds to a black-and-white doctrine of good and evil; that treats questions about its doctrine as a reflection of the skeptic's imperfection; that encourages members to feel part of an elite group whose leaders are seen as perfect. The book also described how cults pressure their members into cutting off contact with family and friends, and how cult leaders encourage members to shun those who question the leaders' authority. My heart stopped when I read that description—I didn't want it to fit The Group, but it did.

When I finally decided to sue, I couldn't wait to face Mary and Margaret and tell them how they'd hurt me. But there was also a part of me that wanted to apologize for having brought them there. I still longed for the sense of community and belonging I'd felt in The Group. The emotions we had experienced together were so intense that I had felt bonded with these people for life, as though we were survivors of a plane crash.

When I started my testimony, however, I gained strength as I told the truth about what had happened to me—and watched Mary and Margaret lie. They said they had never encouraged me to detach myself from my parents. They said they'd never encouraged or believed any of my flashbacks. They said they'd never told me to flee and change my identity. They said they had never controlled people's diets, or their sex lives, or called us abusive names like "slut" and "cult whore." While they denied the charges and gave their own version of the events, I had to endure the indignity of having all thirteen of my personal diaries—now exhibits for the defense—photocopied and passed around to lawyers on the other side. I had to listen as a room full of strangers dissected the details of my therapy, my home life, my pre-Group sex life, with the aim of proving my innate instability. At some points, Mary and Margaret rolled their eyes and laughed at my testimony. But finally, on the morning my case was set to go to trial, their side offered a settlement. I was relieved that I didn't have to testify in court. Though some of their clients reported Mary and Margaret to the state licensing board, resulting in the suspension of their licenses, the last I heard, they were still carrying on with their practice and The Group.

Moving Toward a Life More Ordinary

Two years after the lawsuit, my life is returning to normal, I've completed the two college classes I'd left unfinished and earned my degree. I'm going to massage-therapy school this year, and am enrolled as a graduate student in psychology. I'm sure that seems an odd career choice, but I feel that helping people in an ethical way can be my path toward feeling whole again. When I look back, I know that I was especially vulnerable to The Group: I had zero self-esteem and felt connected to nothing. Finding a place where I felt I belonged was the biggest fulfillment I could imagine. I think that, under the right circumstances, almost anyone could fall prey to a group that promised help, understanding and belonging during a difficult time. What makes me saddest about my experience is that if I had found a good, ethical therapist when I first needed help, I could have saved myself years of pain and confusion. I'm still working through the pain of my experience with Mary and Margaret. But I know that the life I lead from now on is the one that really counts.

Organizations to Contact

The editors have compiled the following list of organizations concerned with the issues debated in this book. The descriptions are derived from materials provided by the organizations. All have publications or information available for interested readers. The list was compiled on the date of publication of the present volume; the information provided here may change. Be aware that many organizations take several weeks or longer to respond to inquiries, so allow as much time as possible.

American Civil Liberties Union (ACLU)
125 Broad St., Eighteenth Fl., New York, NY 10004
(888) 567-ACLU
Web site: www.aclu.org

The American Civil Liberties Union was founded in 1920. The ACLU works in the courts, legislatures, and communities to defend and preserve the individual rights and liberties guaranteed by the Constitution and laws of the United States. The mission of the ACLU is to preserve the following: First Amendment rights such as freedom of speech, freedom of the press, and freedom of religion; the right to equal protection under the law; the right to due process; and the right to privacy.

The Becket Fund for Religious Liberty
1350 Connecticut Ave. NW, Suite 605
Washington, DC 20036
(202) 955-0095
Web site: www.becketfund.org

Becket Fund for Religious Liberty is a Washington, D.C.–based public interest law firm protecting the free expression of all religious traditions. It is nonprofit, nonpartisan, and interfaith.

The Cult Hotline & Clinic
120 W. Fifty-seventh St., New York, NY 10019
(212) 632-4640
e-mail: info@cultclinic.org
Web site: www.cultclinic.org

The Cult Hotline & Clinic was founded in 1980 to serve families and friends of cult members, former cult members, and to educate community groups most at risk of interaction with cults. The clinic is a nonprofit, nonsectarian counseling and education organization working with people of all religious, ethnic, and racial backgrounds. The organization offers a hotline and counseling services for cult members' parents, who are often worried, upset, and confused about what to do. Articles and testimonials from former cult members are available on its Web site.

Cult Information Centre(CIC)
BCM Cults, London, United Kingdom WC1 3XX
Web site: www.cultinformation.org.uk

CIC is an educational charity providing advice and information for victims of cults, their families and friends, researchers, and the media. CIC was founded in 1987 and was the first educational organization focusing critical concern on the harmful methods of cults to be granted charitable status in the United Kingdom. CIC is concerned about the use of deceptive and manipulative methods by cults to recruit and indoctrinate unsuspecting members of society. Its publications include *Cults: A Practical Guide* by Ian Haworth, *Cult Concerns: An Overview of Cults and Their Harmful Methods in the UK* and *Caring for the Family of Cult Victims.*

Cult Information Service, Inc.
Box 867, Teaneck, NJ 07666
(201) 833-1212
e-mail: cultinformationservice@yahoo.com
Web site: www.cultinformationservice.org

Cult Information Service, Inc. is a tax-exempt, nonprofit, educational, self-help organization. It is made up primarily of volunteers and is dedicated to educating the public about the danger and harmful effects of mind control used by destructive cults by providing support and referral to victims and those affected. It also provides information for professionals and people interested in researching destructive cults and cult behavior.

CultsOnCampus
PO Box 11011, Carson, CA 90749
(310) 283-2888
e-mail: cultsoncampus@cultsoncampus.com
Web site: www.cultsoncampus.com

CultsOnCampus.com is an online information site directed at students who are often vulnerable to cults' persuasive tactics. The site offers updated links to cult-related news items, in addition to a list of events on campuses nationwide, books, photographs, videos, and messageboards on cults.

International Cultic Studies Association (ICSA)
PO Box 2265, Bonita Springs, FL 34133
(239) 514-3081
e-mail: mail@icsamail.com
Web site: www.icsahome.com

Founded in 1979, the International Cultic Studies Association is a global network of people concerned about psychological manipulation and abuse in cultic groups, alternative movements, and other environments. In order to help affected families and individuals, enhance the skills of helping professionals, and forewarn those who might become involved in harmful group situations, ICSA collects and disseminates information through periodicals and Web sites, conducts and encourages research, maintains an information phone line, and runs workshops and conferences. ICSA consists of and responds to the needs of people interested in cults, new religious movements, sects, and spiritual abuse. Publications include ICSA *e-Newsletter* and the *Cultic Studies Review.*

Rick A. Ross Institute of New Jersey (RRI)
Newport Financial Center, Jersey City, NJ 07310-1756
(201) 434-9234
e-mail: info@rickross.com
Web site: www.rickross.com

RRI's mission is to study destructive cults and controversial groups and movements and to provide a broad range of information and services easily accessible to the public for assistance and educational purposes. The institute is a nonprofit public resource with an online archive that contains news stories, research papers, reports, court documents, book excerpts, personal testimonies, and links to additional relevant resources.

For Further Research

Books

Eileen Barker, *The Making of a Moonie*. Oxford, UK: Basil Blackwell, 1984.

Derek Daschke and W. Michael Ashcraft, eds., *New Religious Movements: A Documentary Reader*. New York: New York University Press, 2005.

Lorne Dawson, *Comprehending Cults: The Sociology of New Religious Movements*. New York: Oxford University Press, 1998.

Alex Heard, *Apocalypse Pretty Soon: Travels in End-Time America*. New York: Doubleday, 1999.

Philip Jenkins, *Mystics and Messiahs: Cults and New Religions in American History*. New York: Oxford University Press, 2001.

Janja Lalich, *Bounded Choice: True Believers and Charismatic Cults*. Berkeley and Los Angeles: University of California Press, 2004.

Deborah Layton, *Seductive Poison: A Jonestown Survivor's Story of Life and Death in the Peoples Temple*. New York: Anchor/Doubleday, 1998.

Robert Jay Lifton, *Destroying the World to Save It: Aum Shinrikyo, Apocalyptic Violence, and the New Global Terrorism*. New York: Owl Books, 2000.

Michael L. Mickler, *A History of the Unification Church in America, 1959–1974*. New York: Garland, 1993.

Nancy O'Meara, *The Cult Around the Corner: A Handbook on Dealing with Other People's Religions*. Los Angeles: Foundation for Religious Freedom, 2003.

Dick J. Reavis, *The Ashes of Waco: An Investigation*. Syracuse, NY: Syracuse University Press, 1998.

Margaret Singer, *Cults in Our Midst: The Continuing Fight Against Their Hidden Menace*. San Francisco: Jossey-Bass, 2003.

Denice Stephenson, *Dear People: Remembering Jonestown*. Berkeley, CA: Heyday Books, 2005.

David Thibodeau, *A Place Called Waco: A Survivor's Story*. New York: HarperCollins, 1999.

Catherine Wessinger, *How the Millennium Comes Violently: From Jonestown to Heaven's Gate*. New York: Seven Bridges, 2000.

Periodicals

Peter Boyer, "Children of Waco," *New Yorker*, May 15, 1995.

Arian Campo-Flores, "He Calls Himself God," *Newsweek*, February 5, 2007.

Henri Cauvin, "Ugandans Count Cult's Bodies, and Ask Why," *New York Times*, March 21, 2000.

Erik Eckholm, "Boys Cast Out by Polygamists Find New Help," *New York Times*, September 9, 2007.

Steven J. Gelberg, "Some Things I Learned During My Seventeen Years in the Hare Krishna Movement," *ICSA e-Newsletter* vol. 6, no.3, 2007. Available at http://icsahome.com/infoserv_articles.

Eagan Hunter, "Adolescent Attraction to Cults," *Adolescence*, Fall 1998.

Jill Newmark, Marian Jones, and Dennis Gersten, "Crimes of the Soul," *Psychology Today*, March/April 1998.

Stephen Ornes, "Whatever Happened to. . . . EST?" *Discover*, July 2007.

Jennifer E. Porter, "Spirituals, Aliens and UFOs: Extraterrestrials as Spirit Guides," *Journal of Contemporary Religion* October 1996.

Joshua Quitter, "Life and Death on the Web," *Time* April 7, 1997.

Murray Sayles, "Nerve Gas and the Four Noble Truths," *New Yorker*, April 1, 1996.

Adam Szubin, Carl Jensen, and Rod Gregg, "Interacting with 'Cults': A Policing Model," *FBI Law Enforcement Bulletin.* September 2000.

Wendy Wallace, "I Want My Daughter Back." *Times Educational Supplement* April 14, 2000.

Peter Wilkinson, "The Life & Death of the Chosen One," *Rolling Stone*, June 2005.

Index

D

E

F

G

L

M

N

O

P

R

S

T

U

V

W